Best Hikes Bend

HELP US KEEP THIS GUIDE UP TO DATE

Every effort has been made by the author and editors to make this guide as accurate and useful as possible. However, many things can change after a guide is published—regulations change, facilities come under new management, and so forth.

We would love to hear from you concerning your experiences with this guide and how you feel it could be improved and kept up to date. While we may not be able to respond to all comments and suggestions, we'll take them to heart, and we'll also make certain to share them with the author. Please send your comments and suggestions to falconeditorial@rowman.com.

Thanks for your input!

Best Hikes Bend

Simple Strolls, Day Hikes, and Longer Adventures

Second Edition

Lizann Dunegan

ESSEX, CONNECTICUT

FALCONGUIDES®

An imprint of Globe Pequot, the trade division of The Rowman & Littlefield Publishing Group, Inc.
4501 Forbes Blvd., Ste. 200
Lanham, MD 20706
www.rowman.com

Falcon and FalconGuides are registered trademarks and Make Adventure Your Story is a trademark of The Rowman & Littlefield Publishing Group, Inc.

Distributed by NATIONAL BOOK NETWORK

British Library Cataloguing in Publication Information available

Library of Congress Cataloging-in-Publication Data

Names: Dunegan, Lizann, author.
Title: Best hikes Bend : simple strolls, day hikes, and longer adventures / Lizann Dunegan.
Other titles: Best hikes near Bend
Description: Second edition. | Essex, Connecticut : Falcon Guides, [2023]
Identifiers: LCCN 2023002933 (print) | LCCN 2023002934 (ebook) | ISBN 9781493069675
  (paperback) | ISBN 9781493069682 (epub)
Subjects: LCSH: Hiking—Oregon, Central—Guidebooks. | Oregon, Central—Guidebooks.
Classification: LCC GV199.42.O742 D86 2023 (print) | LCC GV199.42.O742 (ebook) | DDC
  796.5109795—dc23/eng/20230202
LC record available at https://lccn.loc.gov/2023002933
LC ebook record available at https://lccn.loc.gov/2023002934

♾™ The paper used in this publication meets the minimum requirements of American National Standard for Information Sciences—Permanence of Paper for Printed Library Materials, ANSI/ NISO Z39.48-1992.

Contents

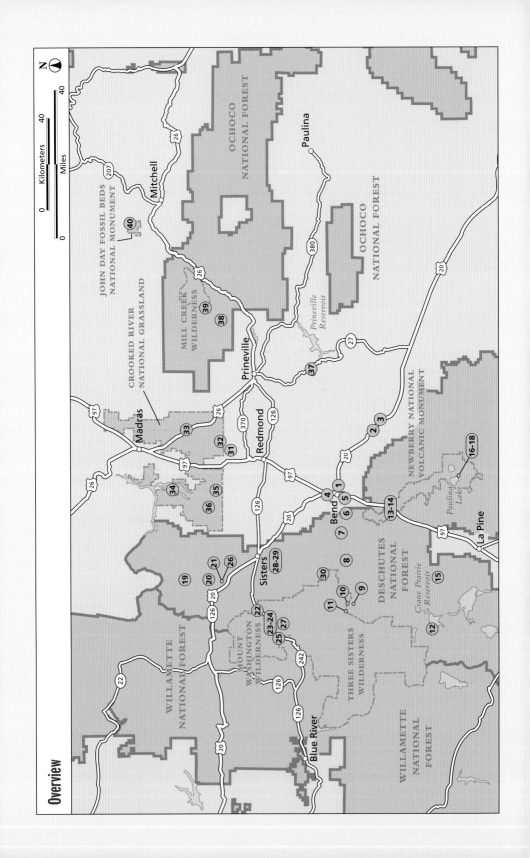

Overview

Acknowledgments

I'd like to thank everyone who helped me research the hikes for this book as well as accompanied me during my trail research, including Ken Skeen and my two canine trail companions Tiz and Zane. Thanks also to the editors at FalconGuides who answered my questions and helped me throughout the writing process.

A majestic bald eagle rests in the branches of a towering pine (hike 15).

Introduction

As Central Oregon's largest city, Bend is a hiker's paradise due to its close proximity to the Deschutes National Forest, Newberry National Volcanic Monument, the Three Sisters Wilderness, and Central Cascade Mountains. Bend Parks and Recreation District is host to sixty-eight parks and more than 65 miles of trails that link many of these parks together, making it one of the most hikable cities in Oregon. The Deschutes River runs through the center of Bend's amazing web of urban trails, and there are many hiking trails in this book where you can hike along different sections of this scenic river within Bend's city limits.

Bend has something to offer all types of hikers both within Bend's city limits and in the surrounding area. This guidebook includes some of the best trails within 2 hours of Bend's downtown, including hikes in and around Sisters, Redmond, and Prineville. The guide lists easy, moderate, and challenging hikes that will appeal to new and veteran hikers.

Weather

Unlike the Willamette Valley to the west, Bend and Central Oregon is much sunnier and dryer. The average rainfall in this part of the state is about 12 inches, and blue skies are the norm. Summers are hot, and winters are cold. Summer temperatures range from the mid-70s to low 90s. Winter temperatures can range from the mid-20s to mid-50s. Be prepared for a substantial amount of snow in the high mountain areas above 4,000 feet and periodic snow showers at lower elevations. Hikes at elevations above 4,000 feet may not be accessible until late June to early July.

Flora and Fauna

Central Oregon is host to the beautiful Deschutes National Forest, Three Sisters Wilderness, Mount Washington Wilderness, Newberry National Volcanic Monument, Ochoco National Forest, and Bureau of Land Management public lands, all of which are home to a wide variety of plant and animal species. At elevations of 5,000 to 7,500 feet, you will typically find mountain hemlock and subalpine fir. In areas where the tree canopy is dense, you will not find many grasses or shrubs. In more open areas you'll find woodrush, grouse huckleberry, and lupine. Wildlife you might see at this elevation includes gray jays, blue grouse, Clark's nutcrackers, snowshoe hares, and American martens.

Nice mountain views on the Canyon Creek Meadows Trail (hike 26).

At elevations of 3,000 to 7,000 feet, you will typically find a mixed conifer forest, which may include white fir, Douglas fir, ponderosa pine, western larch, and lodgepole pine. In mixed conifer forests with more of an open canopy, you'll find shrubs such as manzanita, chinquapin, ceanothus, snowberry, and vine maple. The northern goshawk, Cooper's hawk, and sharp-shinned hawk nest in secluded tree thickets. These hawks hunt small bird and mammal prey through the dense foliage. The pileated woodpecker may also be seen here in the abundant large snags that they prefer for nesting and foraging. Bald eagles and ospreys can be seen along streams and near lakes. Black bears and Rocky Mountain elk can typically be seen at these elevations.

In the canyons, valleys, and plateaus of Central Oregon at lower elevations (typically 3,000 to 4,300 feet), the dominant tree species is the western juniper. This part of the state is home to the second-largest juniper forest in the world. The western juniper grows well in the hot sun and can thrive on less than 8 inches of rain per year. In the dry juniper landscape, you will also find big sagebrush, antelope bitterbrush, fescue, and blue bunch wheatgrass. Poplars and cottonwoods flourish along rivers and streams. These fast-growing trees are a common sight on farms and ranches where they provide shade and serve as windbreaks. Wildflowers like purple lupine, Indian paintbrush, yarrow, and yellow balsamroot add splashes of color to the landscape.

Common animal species include red-tailed hawks, coyotes, jackrabbits, western fence lizards, sagebrush lizards, porcupines, rattlesnakes, quail, and mule deer. In rivers and streams you will often see mallard ducks and Canada geese as well as the rare and elusive river otter.

Wilderness Restrictions/Regulations

The hikes in this guide are found in city parks, state parks, national forests and grasslands, national monuments, wilderness areas, and public lands managed by the Bureau of Land Management (BLM). The Bend Parks and Recreation District manages the parks and trails in and around Bend and has a comprehensive website that contains park and trail maps and park rules and regulations (bendparksandrec .org).

The vast Deschutes National Forest is host to many of the trails in this guide, and some trails described here require a Northwest Forest Pass, which can be obtained for a small fee. For information on purchasing a Northwest Forest Pass, visit www.fs.usda.gov/main/r6/passes-permits/recreation or call (800) 270-7504. You can purchase a daily pass or an annual pass. Hikes in wilderness areas require a free self-issue wilderness permit, which can be obtained at trailheads.

Showy bear grass flowers bloom along the trail (hike 26).

The Newberry National Volcanic Monument charges an entrance fee to enter the monument. You can purchase a day pass at the entrance booth.

Hikes that are in areas managed by the Bureau of Land Management and in the Crooked River National Grassland do not have any permits or fees.

Pilot Butte State Park does not charge an entrance fee, whereas Smith Rock State Park charges a daily entrance fee. A day pass can be purchased at the Smith Rock State Park parking area. You can also purchase an annual state park pass if you plan on visiting more Oregon state parks. Purchase a pass over the phone by calling (800) 551-6949, or, to find a list of vendors that sell Oregon state park passes, visit stateparks.oregon.gov/index.cfm?do=visit.day-use.

How to Use This Guide

Take a close look and you'll find that this guide contains just about everything you'll ever need to choose, plan for, enjoy, and survive a hike near Bend. *Best Hikes Bend* features forty mapped and cued hikes. All the hikes listed in this guide are within 2 hours of Bend. The hikes are organized first by those in and around Bend and then by those located closest to Central Oregon's other cities of Sisters, Redmond, and Prineville.

Each hike starts with a short summary of the hike's highlights. These quick overviews give you a taste of the hiking adventures to follow. You'll learn about the trail terrain and what unique features each trail has to offer.

Following the overview are the hike specs, which contain the quick details of the hike. Here's what you'll find:

Start: This locates the trailhead.

Distance: The total distance of the recommended route—one way for loops or round-trip for out-and-back sections of the trail. Options detail alternate routes along the given hike. The options may shorten the route or describe spur trails to add more highlights (and distance) to the hike.

Hiking time: The average time it will take to cover the route. It is based on the total distance, elevation gain, and condition and difficulty of the trail. Your fitness level will also affect your time.

Difficulty: Each hike has been assigned a level of difficulty. The rating system was developed from several sources and personal experience. These levels are meant to be a guideline only—hikes may prove easier or harder for different people depending on ability and physical fitness.

Easy: 5 miles or less total trip distance in one day, with minimal elevation gain and paved or smooth-surfaced dirt trail.

Moderate: up to 10 miles total trip distance in one day, with moderate elevation gain and potentially rough terrain.

Difficult: more than 10 miles total trip distance in one day, with strenuous elevation gain and rough and/or rocky terrain.

Trail surface: General information about what to expect underfoot.

Best season: General information on the best time of year to hike this route.

Other trail users: Such as horseback riders, mountain bikers, and trail runners.

Canine compatibility: Lists info about taking your dog on each hike. All the hikes in this guide allow dogs. However, some hikes are not recommended for dogs due to intense heat in the summer, rough trail terrain, and/or availability of water.

Land status: Lists if this hike is located in a city park, state park, national forest, wilderness area, national monument, BLM (Bureau of Land Management) lands, or Crooked River National Grassland.

Nearest town: Closest town where you can stock up on groceries, supplies, water, and gas.

Fees and permits: Indicates whether you need to purchase permits or pay park entrance fees.

Schedule: Season, days, and hours that trails are accessible.

Maps: This is a list of other maps to supplement the maps in this book.

Trail contact: The address, phone number, and website for the local land manager(s) in charge of the trails within the selected hike. Obtain trail access information before you head out on your hike.

Finding the trailhead: This section provides driving directions to the trailhead.

The Hike: It's the author's carefully researched impression of the trail. It often includes area history both natural and human.

Miles and Directions: Contains mileage cues that identify all turns and trail name changes as well as points of interest.

Options: Alternate trail routes are given for many described hikes to make your hiking experience shorter or longer depending on the amount of time you have. Don't feel restricted to the routes and trails that are mapped here. Be adventurous and use this guide as a platform to discover new routes for yourself.

Tumalo Creek flows through the center of Shevlin Park (hike 7).

Sidebars: These include interesting information about the area of the trail that doesn't necessarily pertain to the specific hike but gives you some human or natural tidbit that may pique your interest to explore beyond the simple mechanics of the trek.

Enjoy your time outdoors, and remember to pack out what you pack in.

How to Use the Maps

Overview map: This map shows the location of each hike in the area by hike number.

Route map: This is your primary guide to each hike. It shows accessible roads and trails, points of interest, water, landmarks, and geographical features. It also distinguishes trails from roads, and paved roads from unpaved roads. The selected route is highlighted, and directional arrows point the way.

The scenery along this section of the Deschutes River is outstanding (hike 13).

Trail Finder

Hike No.	Hike Name	Best Hikes for Waterfalls	Best Hikes for Great Views	Best Hikes for Children	Best Hikes for Dogs	Best Hikes for Stream Lovers	Best Hikes for Lake Lovers	Best Hikes for Nature Lovers	Best Hikes for History Lovers
1	Pilot Butte State Park		●						
2	Oregon Badlands Wilderness			●	●			●	
3	Dry River Gorge			●	●			●	
4	Drake Park			●	●	●		●	●
5	Old Mill District—Deschutes River Loop			●	●	●		●	●
6	First Street Rapids Park—Deschutes River Trail		●	●	●	●		●	
7	Shevlin Park Loop			●	●	●		●	●
8	Tumalo Falls	●	●	●		●		●	
9	Ray Atkeson Memorial Trail		●				●	●	●

10	Green Lakes	●	●		●	●	●	●	
11	South Sister		●			●	●	●	
12	Osprey Point			●	●		●	●	
13	Benham Falls—Deschutes River Trail	●	●	●	●	●		●	
14	Lava Lands Visitor Center Trails		●	●				●	
15	Fall River			●	●	●		●	
16	Big Obsidian Flow Trail		●	●				●	●
17	Paulina Peak		●					●	●
18	Paulina Lakeshore Loop		●	●	●	●	●	●	●
19	West Metolius River Trail	●	●	●	●	●		●	

(Continued)

(Continued)

Hike No.	Hike Name	Best Hikes for Waterfalls	Best Hikes for Great Views	Best Hikes for Children	Best Hikes for Dogs	Best Hikes for Stream Lovers	Best Hikes for Lake Lovers	Best Hikes for Nature Lovers	Best Hikes for History Lovers
20	Head of the Metolius River			●		●		●	
21	Black Butte		●		●			●	●
22	Black Crater		●					●	
23	Lava River Trail—Dee Wright Observatory		●	●				●	●
24	Little Belknap Crater		●					●	
25	Hand Lake		●	●	●		●	●	
26	Canyon Creek Meadows		●	●	●	●	●	●	
27	Matthieu Lakes Loop				●		●	●	●
28	Whychus Creek	●	●	●	●	●		●	
29	Whychus Canyon Preserve				●	●		●	●
30	Tam McArthur Rim		●		●			●	

	C1	C2	C3	C4	C5	C6	C7	C8
31 Smith Rock State Park	•	•		•			•	
32 Gray Butte					•	•	•	
33 Rimrock Springs Natural Area		•			•	•		
34 Tam-a-lau Trail	•	•	•		•	•	•	
35 Steelhead Falls		•		•	•	•	•	•
36 Alder Springs		•		•	•	•	•	
37 Chimney Rock		•			•	•	•	
38 Steins Pillar		•			•	•	•	
39 Twin Pillars—Mill Creek Wilderness	•	•		•	•	•		
40 Painted Hills Unit—John Day Fossil Beds	•	•				•	•	

Map Legend

Transportation

=⟨26⟩= US Highway

=⟨22⟩= State Highway

=⟨57⟩= County/Forest/Local Road

= = = = Unpaved Road

|——+——| Railroad

---·—·— County Line

Trails

------ Featured Trail

—————— Paved Trail

------ Trail

Water Features

Body of Water

Glacier

Lava

River or Creek

Intermittent Stream

Land Management

National Forest/Park/
Wilderness Area

State/County Park

National Monument/
Grassland/Wildlife Area

Symbols

Boat Ramp

Boardwalk

Bridge

Building/Point of Interest

Campground

○ City/Town

Gate

1.3 Mileage Marker

▲ Mountain/Peak

Overlook/Viewpoint

P Parking

Pass/Gap

Picnic Area

Restroom

Spring

① Trailhead

❓ Visitor/Information Center

Waterfall

1 Pilot Butte State Park

This popular hike takes you to the summit of Pilot Butte—a prominent cinder cone and landmark in downtown Bend. You will follow the scenic Bob Bristol Nature Trail 480 feet to the summit where you'll have fantastic views of Mount Bachelor, the Three Sisters, Broken Top, Black Butte, and many other Cascade peaks. There are additional trail options in this park. You can follow the Base Trail, which is a mile-long trail that circles the base of Pilot Butte, and you also have the option of hiking 3.4 miles out-and-back on the Larkspur Trail, which takes you to the Bend Senior Center and Larkspur Park. You can also follow an alternate summit trail that parallels the paved road to the summit or walk on the jogging track in the park.

Start: South end of the main parking area in Pilot Butte State Park
Distance: 1.8-mile out-and-back
Hiking time: 1 to 1.5 hours
Difficulty: Moderate due to elevation gain to the summit of Pilot Butte
Trail surface: Paved trail and dirt path
Best season: Year-round; snow may be present during the winter months
Other trail users: Runners

Canine compatibility: Leashed dogs permitted
Land status: State park
Nearest town: Bend
Fees and permits: None
Schedule: Dawn to dusk
Maps: USGS Pilot Butte
Trail contact: Oregon Parks and Recreation Department, 725 Summer St. NE, Ste. C, Salem; (541) 388-6055; stateparks. oregon.gov

Finding the trailhead: From NE Third Street/US 97 (Business) in Bend, turn east onto Greenwood Avenue/US 20. Continue 1.4 miles and turn left onto NE Azure Drive at the second Pilot Butte Trailhead sign. Follow the signs another 0.3 mile to a large parking area and trailhead. GPS: N44 03.469' / W121 16.706'

The Hike

Pilot Butte State Park has a small system of trails that will satisfy all types of hikers. This hike takes you on the Bob Bristol Nature Trail, which winds to the 4,138-foot summit of Pilot Butte. Pilot Butte is an extinct cinder cone and is a well-known Central Oregon landmark. This route starts at the base of the butte where you will find restrooms with water, picnic tables, and a walking track. Follow the well-graded trail as it winds around the butte at a fairly steep pace. The trail is shaded in spots by native western juniper, which is the most common tree that grows on the butte. Sagebrush, blue bunch wheatgrass, and Idaho fescue can also be seen growing on the butte. In the spring you may see wildflowers blooming, such as rock cress, yarrow, paintbrush, lupine, penstemon, and mariposa lily. Rest benches and

Ken Skeen and Bear hiking on the summit trail.

interpretive signs are interspersed along the trail if you want to take a break. Once you arrive at the summit, you can enjoy a 360-degree view of downtown Bend and Mount Bachelor, the Three Sisters, Broken Top, and other Central Cascade peaks. After you soak in the views, retrace the same route back to the parking area.

This park is also popular with trail runners who test their speed and endurance in the annual trail run race that starts at the base of the butte and goes to the summit. This race is held at the end of September. There is a sign at the trailhead that lists the winning times for each age group.

Miles and Directions

0.0 Start hiking on the paved path accessed from the south end of the main parking area. (See Options for other trails in the park that begin from this parking area.)

0.1 Turn right onto the signed Bob Bristol Nature Trail, which climbs to the 4,138-foot summit of Pilot Butte.

A hiker walking to the summit.

0.9 Arrive at the paved summit road. Continue straight, then cross the summit road and walk up the steps to the summit viewpoint. After soaking in the views, retrace your footsteps down Pilot Butte.

1.8 Arrive back at the trailhead.

Options

Pilot Butte State Park has other trail options. If you don't feel like climbing to the summit, you can follow the mile-long Base Trail, circling the base of the butte. If you are looking for a longer hike, you can follow the paved Larkspur Trail, which takes you 1.7 miles one way to the Bend Senior Center and Larkspur Park.

Nice view of Pilot Butte summit.

Hike Information

Local Information: Visit Bend, 750 NW Lava Rd., Ste. 160, Bend; (877) 245-8484; visitbend.com

Local Events and Attractions: High Desert Museum, 59800 S. Hwy. 97, Bend; (541) 382-4754; highdesertmuseum.org

Restaurants: Worthy Brewing, 495 NE Bellevue Dr., Bend; (541) 639-4776; worthy.beer

GREEN TIP
Recycle your old gear by giving it to an individual or
an organization that will reuse it.

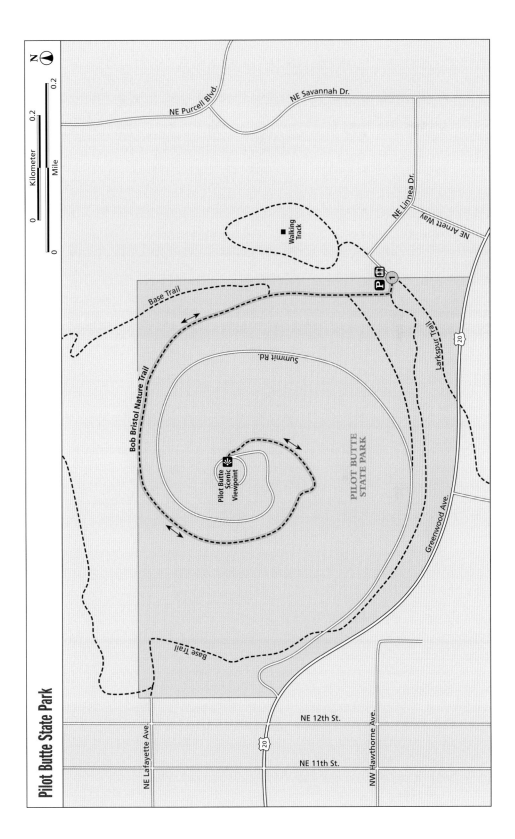

Pilot Butte State Park

N

Kilometer
0   0.2

Mile
0   0.2

NE Purcell Blvd.

NE Savannah Dr.

NE Linnea Dr.

NE Arnett Way

Walking Track

Base Trail

Bob Bristol Nature Trail

Summit Rd.

Larkspur Trail

Pilot Butte Scenic Viewpoint

PILOT BUTTE STATE PARK

Greenwood Ave.

20

Base Trail

NE 12th St.

NE 11th St.

NE Lafayette Ave.

NW Hawthorne Ave.

20

P

1

2 Oregon Badlands Wilderness

This route explores the Flatiron Trail and the Ancient Juniper Trail in the Oregon Badlands Wilderness. The hike takes you through a high desert landscape of old-growth juniper to the summit of Flatiron Rock where you'll enjoy spectacular views of the Central Oregon Cascades. After soaking in the views, you return on the Flatiron Trail to the turnoff to the Ancient Juniper Trail, where you complete a loop through more spectacular old-growth juniper.

Start: Flatiron Rock Trailhead off US 20
Distance: 6.6-mile figure eight
Hiking time: 2.5 to 3.5 hours
Difficulty: Easy due to flat, sandy trail
Trail surface: Dirt and sand trail
Best season: Sept through May
Other trail users: Horseback riders
Canine compatibility: Dogs permitted
Land status: Bureau of Land Management
Nearest town: Bend

Fees and permits: None
Schedule: Open all hours
Maps: USGS Horse Ridge; online map: www.blm.gov/sites/blm.gov/files/documents/files/PRI_BadlandsWilderness_map_0.pdf
Trail contact: Bureau of Land Management, Prineville District Office, 3050 NE Third St., Prineville; (541) 416-6700; www.blm.gov/office/prineville-district-office

Finding the trailhead: From the intersection of US 97 (Business) and US 20, travel 15.8 miles east of downtown Bend on US 20. Turn left into the signed Flatiron Rock Trailhead. GPS: N43 57.46' / W121 3.115'

The Hike

The Oregon Badlands Wilderness is a unique wilderness habitat that covers 29,180 acres and has over 50 miles of trails to explore. Local citizens rallied and supported Senator Ron Wyden when he introduced the Oregon Badlands Wilderness Act in June 2008, and in March 2009 the Oregon Badlands Wilderness Act was signed into law by President Barack Obama.

This wilderness features a vast, western juniper forest sprinkled with the fragrant-smelling sagebrush, rabbitbrush, and bitterbrush and interesting geologic formations. Wildlife you may see in this wilderness area includes red-tailed hawks, ravens, quail, coyotes, bobcats, jackrabbits, mule deer, pronghorn antelope, and elk.

This route flanks the edge of the Badlands shield volcano and takes you to the rocky outcropping known as Flatiron Rock. Once you reach this interesting rock outcropping, you can explore a short loop trail that gives you a different perspective of this unique rock formation. On the return trip you can loop back to the trailhead on the Ancient Juniper Trail, which circles through more of the ancient juniper forest that is the centerpiece of this high desert region. This area is very hot and dry in the summer months, and it is a good idea to bring extra water.

Ken Skeen, Bear, and Tiz take a break on the Flatiron Trail in the Oregon Badlands Wilderness.

From the top of Flatiron Rock you have gorgeous views of Mount Bachelor, Broken Top, and the Three Sisters Mountains.

Miles and Directions

0.0 Start hiking on the Flatiron Trail, which heads to the right.

1.2 Arrive at the junction with Ancient Juniper Trail. Continue straight (right).

1.3 Arrive at the junction with the Homestead Trail. Continue straight (left).

2.8 Arrive at a three-way trail junction. Turn left and start hiking the trail to the top of Flatiron Rock. (The Flatiron Trail continues straight, and the Castle Trail goes right at this junction.) Once you reach the top, enjoy the views and complete a small loop that tours Flatiron Rock. Once you complete the loop, return to the Castle Trail/Flatiron Trail junction.

3.1 Turn right onto the Flatiron Trail.

4.7 Arrive at the junction with the Ancient Juniper Trail and turn right.

6.6 Arrive back at the trailhead.

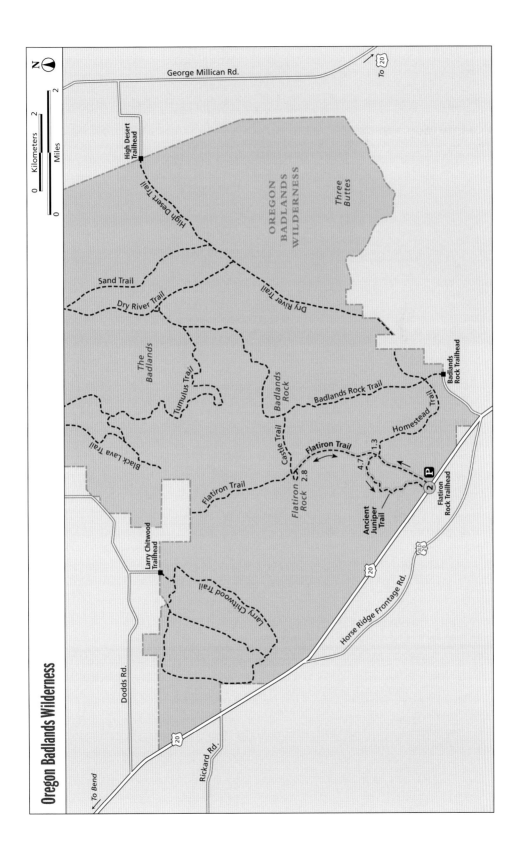

Oregon Badlands Wilderness

N

Kilometers
0   2

Miles
0   2

To Bend

Dodds Rd.

Rickard Rd.

Larry Chitwood Trailhead

Larry Chitwood Trail

Black Lava Trail

Flatiron Trail

Tumulus Trail

Sand Trail

Dry River Trail

High Desert Trail

High Desert Trailhead

George Millican Rd.

To 20

OREGON
BADLANDS
WILDERNESS

Three
Buttes

The
Badlands

Castle Trail

Badlands
Rock

Badlands Rock Trail

Badlands Rock Trailhead

Flatiron Trail 2.8

Flatiron
Rock

Flatiron Trail

Homestead Trail

4.7

1.3

Ancient
Juniper
Trail

P

2 Flatiron Rock Trailhead

20

OLD 20

20

Horse Ridge Frontage Rd.

Old-growth juniper on the Ancient Juniper Trail.

Hike Information

Local Information: Visit Bend, 750 NW Lava Rd., Ste. 160, Bend; (877) 245-8484; visitbend.com

Restaurants: Worthy Brewing, 495 NE Bellevue Dr., Bend; (541) 639-4776; worthy.beer

"POLKA-DOTS ON THE HILLSIDES"

Western juniper trees blanket the Central Oregon region—prompting the description in this headline—and make up the second-largest juniper forest in the world. Western junipers grow well in the hot sun and can thrive on less than 8 inches of rain per year. The small, fragrant, bluish berries of the juniper are a favorite food of small mammals and birds.

3 Dry River Gorge

This hike explores an ancient river gorge and passes through an old-growth juniper forest, affording many opportunities to see ravens, hawks, and other wildlife.

Start: Dry River Canyon trailhead at road's end
Distance: 6.0-mile out-and-back
Hiking time: 2.5 to 3.5 hours
Difficulty: Easy due to fairly flat terrain
Trail surface: Dirt and sand trail
Best season: Open Feb 1 through Aug 31
Other trail users: Horseback riders and mountain bikers
Canine compatibility: Dogs permitted
Land status: Bureau of Land Management

Nearest town: Bend
Fees and permits: None
Schedule: Open Feb 1 through Aug 31
Maps: USGS Horse Ridge; online map: www.blm.gov/sites/blm.gov/files/documents/files/PRI_BadlandsWilderness_map_0.pdf
Trail contact: Bureau of Land Management, Prineville District Office, 3050 NE Third St., Prineville; (541) 416-6700; www.blm.gov/office/prineville-district-office

Finding the trailhead: From Bend head east on US 20 to milepost 17. From milepost 17 continue 0.5 mile and turn right onto a doubletrack dirt road. Cross a cattle guard and turn right into the ODOT gravel storage area. If you have a low-clearance vehicle, you may want to park here at the information kiosk. Continue another 0.9 mile on a rough doubletrack road to the road's end. GPS: N43 56.247' / W121 1.04'

The Hike

This route follows the course of a prehistoric river through a magnificent rocky gorge and is part of the Oregon Badlands Wilderness. The river that once flowed here drained a large ice lake, which formed east of the gorge when lava flows created a natural dam. During episodes of high rainfall, the lake would overflow over a low pass located at the eastern edge of Horse Ridge. This strong, coursing flow of water cut through the porous lava, creating this scenic river gorge. The river flowed north and eventually drained into the Crooked River. Groups of Native Americans camped around this ancient lake, and pictographs have been found on the rocks in the gorge.

This out-and-back hike takes you deep into the canyon, which is filled with old-growth western juniper trees and fragrant sagebrush and rabbitbrush. During the spring months delicate wildflowers add splashes of color to the trail.

As you walk along the trail, you'll be amazed by the bright lime-green and orange lichens that cover the canyon walls. These high rimrock canyon walls are a perfect place for ravens and raptors to nest. At 0.9 mile and 2.2 miles you'll pass old-growth ponderosa pines that have managed to survive in this very dry canyon. At 2.5 miles the trail seems to abruptly come to an end. You have the option of turning around here, or, if you are feeling adventurous and don't mind scrambling over rocks, you can continue on the trail. After you scramble over several large boulders on the right, you'll see the continuation of the rocky trail that has been carved into the right side of the canyon. Follow the trail for 0.1 mile and then descend to the canyon floor. From here the sandy trail continues in a southeast direction. Continue for another 0.4 mile to the trail's end at the opposite end of the canyon.

As you are hiking in the canyon, be on the lookout for rattlesnakes that sometimes make an appearance.

Old-growth juniper tree.

Miles and Directions

0.0 Start by walking south on the main doubletrack road. Turn right at a road junction; you'll continue walking on a doubletrack road for 0.3 mile.

0.3 The wide doubletrack road ends next to a primitive campsite. Continue hiking on a singletrack trail that heads into the canyon.

2.5 Arrive at a large boulder field where the trail seems to end. (***Option:*** Turn around here.) Continue on the trail by scrambling over a series of boulders on your right and hiking on a rocky path. The path goes for 0.1 mile and then descends to the canyon floor.

2.6 The rocky section ends. Continue your journey up the canyon on a smooth sandy trail.

3.0 Arrive at the end of the trail and your turnaround point at the end of the canyon. Retrace the same route back to the trailhead.

6.0 Arrive back at the trailhead.

Hike Information

Local Information: Visit Bend, 750 NW Lava Rd., Ste. 160, Bend; (877) 245-8484; visitbend.com

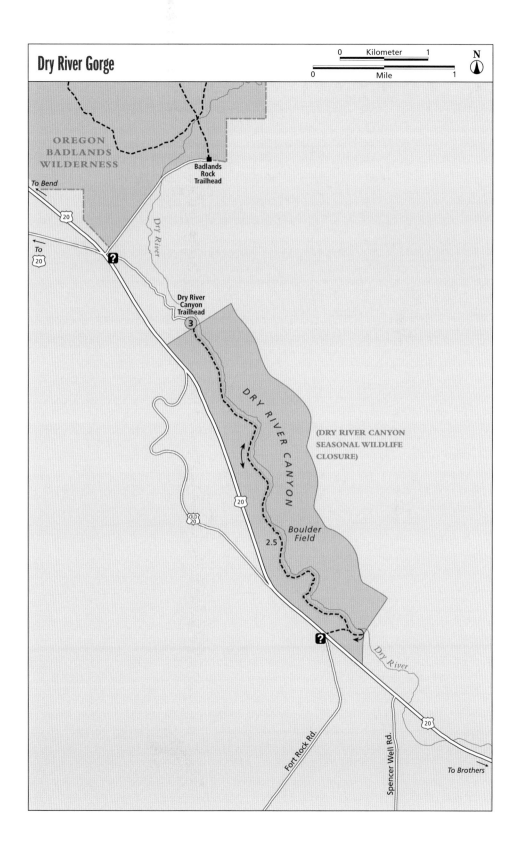

Dry River Gorge

0   Kilometer   1
0   Mile   1

N

OREGON
BADLANDS
WILDERNESS

To Bend

20

To
20

Badlands
Rock
Trailhead

Dry River

Dry River
Canyon
Trailhead

3

DRY RIVER CANYON

(DRY RIVER CANYON
SEASONAL WILDLIFE
CLOSURE)

20

OLD
20

Boulder
Field

2.5

Dry River

Fort Rock Rd.

Spencer Well Rd.

20

To Brothers

4 Drake Park

This easy hike takes you through historic Drake Park in downtown Bend. This picturesque park is filled with towering ponderosa pine trees and parallels Mirror Pond, which is fed by the Deschutes River. The park is host to many events during the year and is a great introduction to Bend's downtown district.

Start: Public parking area off NW Riverside Boulevard in Drake Park
Distance: 0.7-mile loop
Hiking time: 30 minutes to 1 hour
Difficulty: Easy due to flat trail surface
Trail surface: Paved path
Best season: Year-round; snow may be present during the winter months
Other trail users: Runners and cyclists

Canine compatibility: Leashed dogs permitted
Land status: City park
Nearest town: Bend
Fees and permits: None
Schedule: Open 5 a.m. to 10 p.m.
Maps: USGS Bend
Trail contact: Bend Parks and Recreation, 799 SW Columbia St., Bend; (541) 389-7275; www.bendparksandrec.org

Finding the trailhead: At the intersection of US 97 and NW Franklin Avenue in downtown Bend, turn west onto NW Franklin Avenue. Drive 0.8 mile on NW Franklin Avenue (which turns into NW Riverside Boulevard) to a public parking area on the right side of the road in Drake Park. GPS: N43 3.532' / W121 18.947'

The Hike

Drake Park in downtown Bend is a gorgeous city park filled with towering ponderosa pine trees and grassy lawns, and is adjacent to Mirror Pond, which is fed by the Deschutes River. This park is host to numerous events throughout the year and is a popular spot for residents and visitors. Drake Park is named after Alexander M. Drake, who arrived from Michigan in 1900 and was one of the early settlers in this area and responsible for much of the area's development. The park was established in May 1920.

Start the hike at the north end of the parking area by following the paved path as it parallels the Deschutes River and Mirror Pond. As you hike you'll find many interpretive signs that tell stories of some of the settlers who lived here.

You will also see Canada geese and mallard ducks swimming and feeding in the quiet waters of Mirror Pond. At 0.2 mile you'll pass a restroom on the left. Continue to hike on the paved path at the water's edge until you reach a bridge that spans the river. At the bridge go left and loop back to your starting point on a paved path that winds through stately ponderosa pines. At 0.6 mile you will pass a historic high-wheel log skidder. Log skidders were pulled by a team of four draft horses and loaded with one to three 16-foot logs and hauled to a landing where the logs could

Drake Park is located in Bend's downtown core and is a popular destination with locals and visitors alike.

then be loaded onto a railcar for transport to the closest lumber mill. At 0.7 mile you'll arrive back at your starting point.

After the hike you may want to explore the shops in downtown Bend and visit one of the local breweries listed under Restaurants for this hike.

This high-wheel log skidder at mile 0.6 carried logs to a railcar for transport to a lumber mill.

Miles and Directions

0.0 Start hiking on the paved path along the Deschutes River that starts at the north end of the parking lot.

0.2 Pass a restroom on the left.

Mallard ducks are a common sight in Drake Park.

0.4 Reach a bridge that spans the river and a three-way junction. Turn left and follow the paved path as it loops back through the park.

0.6 Pass a high-wheel log skidder and interpretive sign.

0.7 Arrive back at your starting point.

Hike Information

Local Information: Visit Bend, 750 NW Lava Rd., Ste. 160, Bend; (877) 245-8484; visitbend.com

Local Events and Attractions: High Desert Museum, 59800 S. Hwy. 97, Bend; (541) 382-4754; highdesertmuseum.org

Restaurants: Bend Brewing Company, 1019 NW Brooks St., Bend; (541) 383-1599; bendbrewingco.com

Crux Fermentation Project, 50 SW Division St., Bend; (541) 385-3333; cruxfermentation.com

Deschutes Brewery, 1044 NW Bond St., Bend; (541) 382-9242; deschutesbrewery.com

10 Barrel Brewing, 1135 NW Galveston, Bend; (541) 678-5228; 10barrel.com

FARMERS' MARKET

Bend Farmers Market is becoming one of Oregon's leading farm-direct marketplaces, bringing together growers and producers with people who hunger for fresh, local, healthful foods and agricultural goods. Every Wednesday afternoon from 2 to 6 p.m. May 4 through October 12, you can visit the local farmers' market held in Drake Park. Note that dogs are not allowed. For more Information contact Bend Farmers Market, PO Box 123, Bend, OR 97709; (541) 408-4998; bendfarmersmarket.com.

CANADA GEESE

Be on the lookout for the Canada geese that can be seen feeding and swimming in Mirror Pond. They migrate through the Pacific Northwest on their way to Mexico, and some stay to become year-round residents. They have a gray body, black head and throat, and white patches on their face and chest. They feed on grasses and aquatic plants and animals and can be seen in lakes, ponds, rivers, and marshes. They also feed on grains and are attracted to farmers' fields that have just been harvested. These majestic birds have a sophisticated mating ritual and mate for life.

GREEN TIP
Never feed wild animals under any circumstances.
You may damage their health and expose yourself
(and them) to danger.

Drake Park

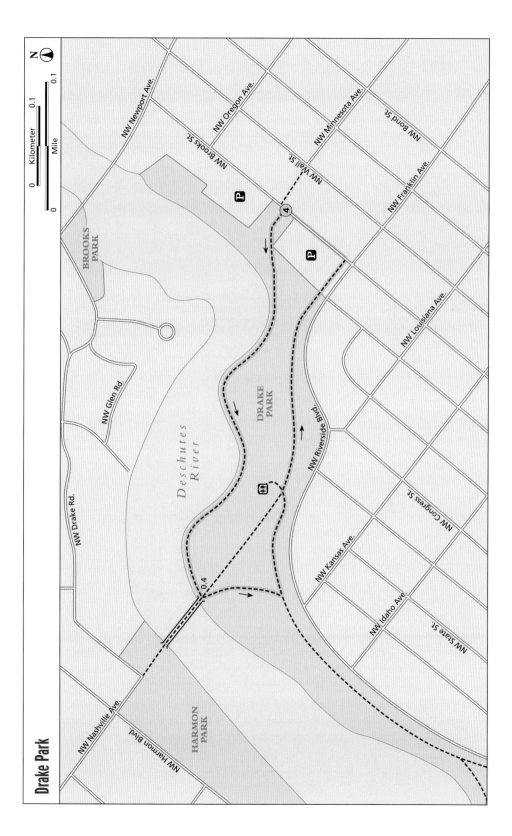

N

0   Kilometer   0.1   0.1

0   Mile   0.1

BROOKS PARK

NW Glen Rd.

NW Drake Rd.

Deschutes River

DRAKE PARK

NW Riverside Blvd.

NW Nashville Ave.

NW Harmon Blvd.

HARMON PARK

NW State St.

NW Idaho Ave.

NW Kansas Ave.

NW Congress St.

NW Louisiana Ave.

NW Franklin Ave.

NW Bond St.

NW Minnesota Ave.

NW Wall St.

NW Oregon Ave.

NW Brooks St.

NW Newport Ave.

4

0.4

P

P

5 Old Mill District–Deschutes River Loop

This scenic river hike takes you along the banks of the Deschutes River in the Old Mill District—a popular shopping area in Bend. The route starts in Farewell Bend Park and completes a loop past viewpoints of the river where you'll see mallard ducks, Canada geese, and blue herons. If you are hiking with your dog, you will also have an opportunity to visit the leash-free Riverbend Dog Park. Even if you don't have a dog, it's fun to stop and witness pure canine joy. This area has many other hiking options available if you are looking for a longer or shorter hike.

Start: Farewell Bend Park parking area
Distance: 2.7-mile loop
Hiking time: 1 to 2 hours
Difficulty: Easy due to paved paths and well-graded dirt paths
Trail surface: Paved path and dirt path
Best season: Year-round
Other trail users: Runners and cyclists
Canine compatibility: Leashed dogs permitted

Land status: City park
Nearest town: Bend
Fees and permits: None
Schedule: Open 5 a.m. to 10 p.m.
Maps: USGS Bend
Trail contact: Bend Parks and Recreation, 799 SW Columbia St., Bend; (541) 389-7275; www.bendparksandrec.org

Finding the trailhead: From Bend Parkway South in Bend, take exit 139 for Reed Market Road/Old Mill District. At the end of the off-ramp, turn right onto Reed Market Road. Continue 0.5 mile on Reed Market Road and turn right into the Farewell Bend Park parking area that parallels the Deschutes River. GPS: N44 02.451' / W121 19.241'

The Hike

This scenic urban loop hike takes you along the banks of the Deschutes River in the Old Mill District neighborhood and shopping area in southwest Bend. The Old Mill District is a fun shopping center that features a movie theater, retail shops, and many restaurants. If you need to pick up any hiking gear, REI has a large store located in this shopping district.

There are many interpretive signs along this route that describe how logs were once floated down the Deschutes River to be milled into lumber at the lumber mills located on both sides of the river. The Shevlin-Hixon Lumber Company built a sawmill here on the west side of the river in 1916, and the Brooks-Scanlon Lumber Company built Sawmill "A" on the east side of the river the same year. In 1922 Brooks-Scanlon built an additional Sawmill "B" complex. The mills were the center of Bend's economy for many years until the area's lumber resources became depleted. In 1950 the Shevlin-Hixon Mill was purchased by Brooks-Scanlon and shortly thereafter was closed. The Brooks-Scanlon operations dwindled until the final mill closure in 1993. The area was then purchased and redeveloped in the mid-1990s.

Hikers and their dogs enjoying a walk in the Old Mill District.

The hike starts in Farewell Bend Park adjacent to the Deschutes River. Farewell Bend Park covers 22 acres and features a natural marsh and canoe launch. It also features a wildlife viewing ramp to explore at the 0.2-mile mark. It takes you out onto the Deschutes River where you may see mallard ducks, Canada geese, and other birdlife. After 0.4 mile you will cross the Deschutes River and turn north.

The Deschutes River flows wide and slow along this section and is very popular for canoeing, kayaking, and stand-up paddleboarding. After another 0.4 mile you will pass Riverbend Park. This 13.9-acre park provides access to the Deschutes River, has large grassy areas and public restrooms, and also features a fenced, leash-free dog park. If you are interested in exploring the shops and restaurants in the Old Mill District shopping area, you can cross the bridge at 1.1 miles and take a tour of this popular shopping district. After 1.6 miles cross the Deschutes River on a footbridge and then complete the return loop as the path continues along the river's edge.

A nice viewing platform gives you a different perspective of the Deschutes River.

Miles and Directions

0.0   From the parking area, turn left (south) and walk on the paved path.

0.2   Turn right and start walking on a ramp that takes you out to a viewpoint on the river. After enjoying the views, walk back to the main paved path and turn right.

0.4   Turn right and cross a bridge. After crossing the bridge turn right (north). (*Option:* If you are looking for a longer hike, you can turn left and continue south on the Deschutes River Trail.)

0.8   Pass the Riverbend leash-free dog park on the left.

1.0   Turn right and walk through a short tunnel. After going through the tunnel, stay to the right.

1.1   Pass a bridge on the right. You have the option of turning right and going over the bridge to the Old Mill District shops. Continue straight on the paved path.

1.3   Turn right and continue walking on the sidewalk.

1.5   Turn right and onto SW Shevlin Hixon Road and continue walking on the sidewalk.

Old Mill District–Deschutes River Loop

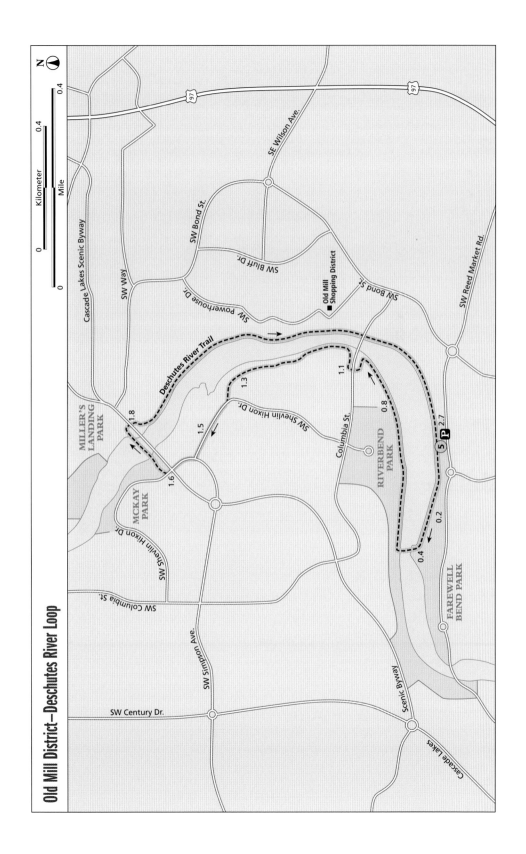

- N
- Kilometer
- Mile
- 0 0.4
- 0 0.4 0.4

Cascade Lakes Scenic Byway

SW Way

SW Bond St.

SW Bluff Dr.

SW Powerhouse Dr.

SE Wilson Ave.

97

97

Old Mill
Shopping District

SW Bond St.

SW Reed Market Rd.

Deschutes River Trail

MILLER'S
LANDING
PARK

1.8

1.6

1.5

1.3

SW Shevlin Hixon Dr.

1.1

Columbia St.

0.8

RIVERBEND
PARK

0.2

0.4

5 P 2.7

FAREWELL
BEND PARK

MCKAY
PARK

SW Shevlin Hixon Dr.

SW Columbia St.

SW Simpson Ave.

SW Century Dr.

Scenic Byway

Cascade Lakes

This viewing ramp leads you out in the middle of the Deschutes River where you can watch for birds and other wildlife.

1.6 Walk under a bridge, then turn right onto the paved path and cross the river on the footbridge.

1.8 After crossing the footbridge, continue straight. Cross NW Industrial Way and then continue on the paved path.

2.4 Walk through the tunnel.

2.7 Arrive back at Farewell Bend Park and your starting point.

Hike Information

Local Information: Visit Bend, 750 NW Lava Rd., Ste. 160, Bend; (877) 245-8484; visitbend.com

Local Events and Attractions: High Desert Museum, 59800 S. Hwy. 97, Bend; (541) 382-4754; highdesertmuseum.org

REI, 380 Powerhouse Dr., Bend; (541) 385-0594; rei.com

Restaurants: Cafe Yumm!, 325 SW Powerhouse Dr., Ste. 130, Bend; (541) 318-9866; cafeyumm.com

6 First Street Rapids Park—Deschutes River Trail

This route takes you along a scenic section of the rambling Deschutes River Trail that begins at First Street Rapids Park in downtown Bend. The trail parallels the river's edge and follows it north through a mix of juniper, sage, and ponderosa pine trees. The last half of this route winds high on the canyon rim and affords stunning views of Mount Washington and Black Butte to the northwest and the Deschutes River far below. There are also options for side trips that you can take on the Upper Sawyer Canyon Trail and the Archie Briggs Canyon Trail.

Start: First Street Rapids Park in downtown Bend

Distance: 7.8-mile out-and-back

Hiking time: 2.5 to 3.5 hours

Difficulty: Easy due to fairly flat trail; some small hills

Trail surface: Graded gravel trail

Best season: Year-round

Other trail users: Runners and cyclists

Canine compatibility: Leashed dogs permitted

Land status: City park

Nearest town: Bend

Fees and permits: None

Schedule: Open 5 a.m. to 10 p.m.

Maps: USGS Bend

Trail contact: Bend Parks and Recreation, 799 SW Columbia St., Bend; (541) 389-7275; www.bendparksandrec.org

Finding the trailhead: From Bend Parkway North in Bend, take exit 137 for Revere Avenue/Downtown Bend. At the end of the off-ramp, turn left onto Revere Avenue and go 0.1 mile. Turn left onto Wall Street. Continue 0.2 mile and turn right onto Portland Avenue. Continue 0.2 mile on Portland Avenue and turn right onto First Street. Continue 0.3 mile to where the street dead-ends at First Street Rapids Park. GPS: N44 4.042' / W121 18.835'

The Hike

First Street Rapids Park is the starting point for this fun route that follows a graded path along the Deschutes River through downtown Bend. This park is a popular put-in spot for kayakers, and you will often see paddlers playing in the water. Watch for small groups of ducks, blue herons, and Canada geese feeding along the riverbank. At 0.7 mile you'll cross Mount Washington Drive and continue on the smooth grade of the well-groomed trail as it continues north. At this point the trail parallels the greens of the River's Edge Golf Course before it enters a forest corridor that passes through several residential areas.

After 1.3 miles you will pass the Upper Sawyer Canyon Trail on the left, which leads to Sawyer Uplands Park. Continue a short distance and then arrive at Robert

First Street Rapids on the Deschutes River.

Sawyer Park. This park covers over 42 acres and is popular for bird-watching. You can cross the Deschutes River on a wood footbridge if you want to explore the other side of the river. There is also a portable restroom located at this park. Over the next 2.6 miles you'll cross two more paved roads as the path winds through an area of expensive homes high above the river. At 2.8 miles you have another opportunity for a side trip to explore the Archie Briggs Canyon Trail. For this hike continue on the Deschutes River Trail. Along this section of the trail, you can see the snowcapped peaks of Mount Washington, Black Butte, and other Central Cascade peaks that dominate the skyline to the west. At 3.9 miles the Deschutes River Trail ends at a green gate where you will turn around and retrace the same route back to the trailhead.

Miles and Directions

0.0 From First Street Rapids Park, begin hiking north on the well-graded trail that parallels the scenic Deschutes River. A portable restroom is available at the trailhead.

0.6 Turn left onto the graded trail (don't go right toward the golf course).

You will have many nice views of the Deschutes River on this route.

0.7   The trail intersects with the paved Mount Washington Drive. Turn right and follow the trail downhill as it parallels Mount Washington Drive. Look for the small Deschutes River Trail signs marking the trail.

0.8   Turn left and cross Mount Washington Drive. Pick up the trail on the other side. Continue on the sidewalk for 0.1 mile.

0.9   Turn left and continue on the graded path.

1.3   Pass the Upper Sawyer Canyon Trail on the left. Continue on the main trail a short distance and then arrive at a trail junction with the signed Robert S. Sawyer Park Trail. Stay to the left and continue on the Deschutes River Trail.

2.0   Cross Archie Briggs Road and continue on the graded trail on the other side.

2.3   Go around a green metal gate.

2.8   The Archie Briggs Canyon Trail goes left. Continue straight on the Deschutes River Trail.

3.9   The Deschutes River Trail ends at a green gate. Turn around and follow the same route back to the trailhead.

7.8   Arrive back at the trailhead.

The fall foliage on the Deschutes River is spectacular.

Hike Information

Local Information: Visit Bend, 750 NW Lava Rd., Ste. 160, Bend; (877) 245-8484; visitbend.com

Local Events and Attractions: High Desert Museum, 59800 S. Hwy. 97, Bend; (541) 382-4754; highdesertmuseum.org

Restaurants: Bend Brewing Company, 1019 NW Brooks St., Bend; (541) 383-1599; bendbrewingco.com

Boneyard Brewing, 1955 NE Division St., Bend; (541) 241-7184; boneyardbeer.com

Crux Fermentation Project, 50 SW Division St., Bend; (541) 385-3333; crux fermentation.com

Deschutes Brewery, 1044 NW Bond St., Bend; (541) 382-9242; deschutesbrewery .com

West Side Bakery & Café, 1005 NW Galveston Ave., Bend; (541) 382-3426; westsidebakeryandcafe.com

CENTRAL OREGON TONGUE TWISTERS

Belknap—BELL-nap	Deschutes—Deh-SHOOTS
Madras—MAD-Russ	Ochoco—O-CHOH-ko
Paulina—Paul-I-nah	

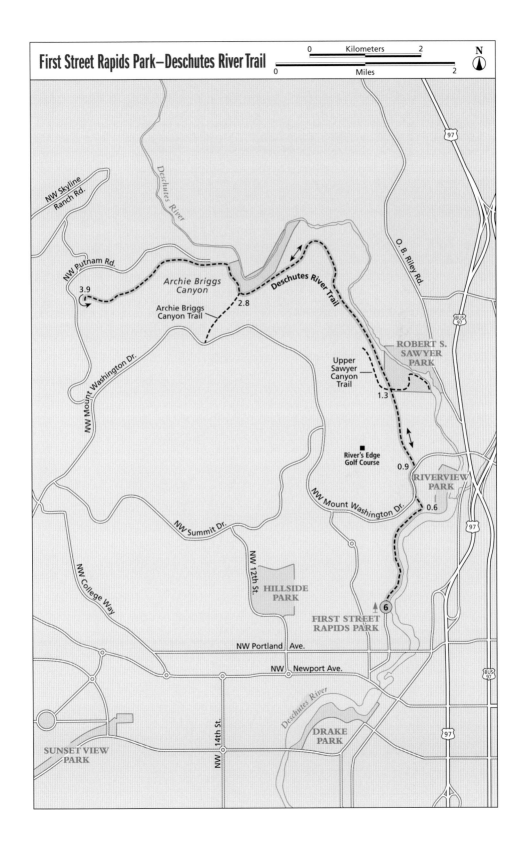

First Street Rapids Park–Deschutes River Trail

Kilometers
0   2

Miles
0   2

N

NW Skyline Ranch Rd.

Deschutes River

O. B. Riley Rd.

97

NW Putnam Rd.

Archie Briggs Canyon

3.9

Deschutes River Trail

2.8

Archie Briggs Canyon Trail

BUS 97

NW Mount Washington Dr.

Upper Sawyer Canyon Trail

ROBERT S. SAWYER PARK

1.3

River's Edge Golf Course

0.9

RIVERVIEW PARK

97

NW Summit Dr.

NW Mount Washington Dr.

0.6

NW College Way

NW 12th St.

HILLSIDE PARK

6

FIRST STREET RAPIDS PARK

NW Portland Ave.

NW Newport Ave.

BUS 97

NW 14th St.

Deschutes River

DRAKE PARK

97

SUNSET VIEW PARK

7 Shevlin Park Loop

This hike is very close to downtown Bend and is a local favorite. The route winds through ponderosa pine and Douglas fir forest along the banks of scenic Tumalo Creek in Shevlin Park.

Start: Shevlin Park's second parking area
Distance: 5.0-mile lollipop loop
Hiking time: 2 to 3 hours
Difficulty: Easy to moderate due to well-graded path with some hill climbing
Trail surface: Graded gravel path and dirt path
Best season: Year-round
Other trail users: Trail runners and mountain bikers

Canine compatibility: Leashed dogs permitted
Land status: City park
Nearest town: Bend
Fees and permits: None
Schedule: Open 5 a.m. to 10 p.m.
Maps: USGS Bend
Trail contact: Bend Parks and Recreation, 799 SW Columbia St., Bend; (541) 389-7275; www.bendparksandrec.org

Finding the trailhead: From Bend Parkway North in Bend, take exit 137 for Revere Avenue/Downtown Bend. At the end of the off-ramp, turn left onto Revere Avenue and go 0.1 mile. Turn left onto Wall Street. Continue 0.2 mile and turn right onto Portland Avenue. Continue 0.7 mile on Portland Avenue and turn left onto 9th Street. Go 1 block and turn right onto Newport Avenue. Continue 3.3 miles on Newport Avenue to the Shevlin Park entrance on the left. Drive through the first parking area and continue 0.1 mile to a second parking area that has a vault toilet. GPS: N44 04.404' / W121 22.885'

The Hike

This route explores the 647-acre Shevlin Park, which was donated by the Shevlin-Hixon Company to the city of Bend in 1920. The park features hiking and mountain biking trails; beautiful Tumalo Creek flows through the center of the park. This park is also very popular with trail runners, who enjoy running on its well-graded paths. Shevlin Park is named for the company's president, Thomas H. Shevlin. At one time Shevlin-Hixon operated one of the largest lumber mills in the country. Its first mill in Bend opened in 1916 and began processing what seemed to be an endless supply of trees. Eventually the tree supply was exhausted. In 1950 Shevlin-Hixon Mill was purchased by Brooks-Scanlon and closed shortly thereafter.

This picturesque hike leads through shimmering aspen trees and stately ponderosa pine trees along the edge of Tumalo Creek. According to Lewis L. McArthur, the author of *Oregon Geographic Names*, the name Tumalo is possibly derived from the word *temolo*, which means "wild plum" in the Klamath tribe language, or the Klamath tribe word *temola*, which translates to "ground fog."

Hikers enjoying the solitude in Shevlin Park.

The path is well graded, and there are many opportunities to stop and admire the creek at one of the many picnic areas scattered along the route. You will cross the creek on footbridges at different points along the way. After 2 miles you'll arrive at historic Fremont Meadow. In 1843, John C. Fremont, an explorer for the US government, and his group camped in this meadow. You also have the opportunity to take a side trip and explore the Shevlin Meadow Interpretive Trail. After 2.4 miles you will cross the creek on the Upper Footbridge and then begin ascending a forested ridge. As you hike the ridge you'll have nice views of the creek canyon. Over the next 2.6 miles the trail takes you along the ridge high above the creek and then descends once again into the creek canyon back to your starting point.

FIRST-AID KIT CHECKLIST FOR YOUR CANINE HIKING PARTNERS

Carry a first-aid kit in the car and on the trail so you are prepared for unforeseen injuries to your canine hiking partner. A good canine first-aid kit should include:

- ☐ Adhesive tape
- ☐ Antibiotic ointment
- ☐ Aspirin
- ☐ Cotton
- ☐ Eyewash
- ☐ Gauze rolls or pads
- ☐ Gloves
- ☐ Hemostats
- ☐ Hydrocortisone ointment
- ☐ Insect sting relief medicated pads
- ☐ Rectal thermometer
- ☐ Scissors, preferably with rounded tips
- ☐ Stretchy leg wrap
- ☐ Syringe (without needle) for giving medications by mouth
- ☐ Tweezers
- ☐ Veterinarian's phone number
- ☐ Veterinary first-aid manual

Miles and Directions

0.0 Start walking on the paved path by the restrooms that heads toward the creek and picnic structure.

0.1 Continue on the dirt path that travels past the picnic shelter. Once you arrive at the creek, turn right onto the well-graded sand/gravel path.

0.7 Arrive at the signed Larch Grove area. Cross a bridge over Tumalo Creek. The trail Ys after crossing the bridge. Go right and continue on the signed Creek Trail. The Shevlin Park Loop Trail goes left.

0.8 Turn right at the trail junction and cross the covered bridge. After crossing the bridge go left and continue on the Creek Trail.

2.0 Arrive at Fremont Meadow. (**Option:** Take a short side trip on the Shevlin Meadow Interpretive Trail, which starts here.) Continue hiking on the Creek Trail.

Tumalo Creek is one of the many highlights on this route.

2.3 Arrive at a three-way junction. Continue straight (left) toward the signed Upper Footbridge.

2.4 Cross the footbridge and continue on the trail as it ascends the ridge.

3.0 Cross a log bridge over a side creek.

3.1 Arrive at a trail junction. Turn left toward the signed Shevlin Park entrance. The Shevlin Park Loop Trail goes right.

3.9 Go left at a T junction. The trail turns into a doubletrack road.

4.1 Turn left toward the Shevlin Park entrance.

4.2 Turn left onto the signed Tumalo Creek Trail and start walking downhill. (The Shevlin Park Loop Trail goes right.)

4.3 Turn right at the trail junction and cross a footbridge over Tumalo Creek.

4.4 The trail intersects with the paved road. Go right and continue hiking on the path.

4.9 Turn left at the trail junction and walk past the picnic shelter.

5.0 Arrive back at the parking area and trailhead.

A unique covered bridge in Shevlin Park.

Hike Information

Local Information: Visit Bend, 750 NW Lava Rd., Ste. 160, Bend; (877) 245-8484; visitbend.com

Local Events and Attractions: High Desert Museum, 59800 S. Hwy. 97, Bend; (541) 382-4754; highdesertmuseum.org

Restaurants: Bend Brewing Company, 1019 NW Brooks St., Bend; (541) 383-1599; bendbrewingco.com

Boneyard Brewing, 37 NW Lake Place, Bend; (541) 323-2325; boneyardbeer.com

Crux Fermentation Project, 50 SW Division St., Bend; (541) 385-3333; cruxfermentation.com

Deschutes Brewery, 1044 NW Bond St., Bend; (541) 382-9242; deschutesbrewery.com

10 Barrel Brewing, 1135 NW Galveston, Bend; (541) 678-5228; 10barrel.com

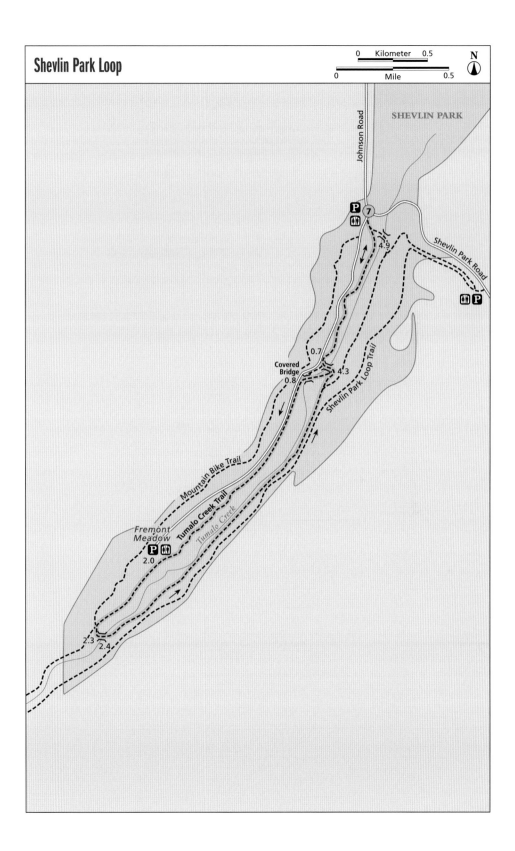

Shevlin Park Loop

Kilometer
0   0.5

Mile
0   0.5

N

Johnson Road

SHEVLIN PARK

P

7

4.9

Shevlin Park Road

P

0.7

Covered
Bridge
0.8

4.3

Shevlin Park Loop Trail

Mountain Bike Trail

Tumalo Creek Trail

Tumalo Creek

Fremont
Meadow
P
2.0

2.3
2.4

8 Tumalo Falls

This route takes you along scenic Tumalo Creek and has many wonderful views of different waterfalls including Tumalo Falls, Double Falls, and Upper Falls. There are additional options for a longer hike to Happy Valley.

Start: Tumalo Falls Trailhead off FR 4603
Distance: 4.4-mile out-and-back
Hiking time: 2 to 3 hours
Difficulty: Moderate due to moderate elevation gain
Trail surface: Dirt path
Best season: May through Oct; snow may be present during the winter months
Other trail users: Runners and mountain bikers (mountain bikers only allowed to ride uphill on this trail)
Canine compatibility: Leashed dogs permitted
Land status: Deschutes National Forest

Nearest town: Bend
Fees and permits: A Northwest Forest Pass is required for a small fee. You can purchase a pass at www.fs.usda.gov/main/deschutes/passes-permits/recreation or by calling (800) 270-7504.
Schedule: Open all hours
Maps: USGS Bend
Trail contact: Deschutes National Forest, Supervisor's Office, 63095 Deschutes Market Rd., Bend; (541) 383-5300; www.fs.usda.gov/main/deschutes/home

Finding the trailhead: From the intersection of NW Galveston Avenue and 14th Street in Bend, follow NW Galveston (which turns into NW Skyliner's Road) for 10 miles. The road Ys and turns to gravel. Turn left onto FR 4603 and follow it for 2.5 miles (the gravel road is washboarded in different sections) to the trailhead. GPS: N44 01.927' / W121 33.990'

The Hike

This route takes you on a tour along Tumalo Creek and past a series of picturesque waterfalls. The Tumalo Creek canyon was carved by glaciers. The source of Tumalo Creek is a series of springs that ensure consistent water flow year-round. About 46 million gallons of Tumalo Creek water is used to irrigate 8,000 acres of farmland each year. In addition, Bridge Creek (a tributary of Tumalo Creek) provides drinking water for Bend residents.

This route is a very popular hike due to its proximity to Bend and its well-groomed trail with many waterfalls. Because of this, it is recommended that you try this hike on a weekday to avoid the weekend crowds.

There are restrooms at the start of this hike and interpretive signs. Start hiking on the signed North Fork Trail as it heads uphill for 0.2 mile to a scenic overlook of 97-foot Tumalo Falls. As you continue on the trail, it winds along the creek's edge through a thick forest of mountain hemlock and Engelmann spruce. At the signed viewpoint at 1.2 miles, you'll have a spectacular view of Double Falls, which follows a curvy path to a twin cascade. Continue another mile up the trail to another

Tumalo Falls is a veil of white dropping into Tumalo Creek.

signed viewpoint of the shimmering cascade of Upper Falls. This is your turnaround point.

You have the option to continue on this trail as it passes more spectacular creek scenery until it intersects with the Swampy Lakes Trail in 1.5 miles. If you turn left onto the Swampy Lakes Trail, you can make a loop. If you want to complete a longer out-and-back hike on the same trail (this option has the best scenery), then at the Swampy Lakes junction stay to the right and hike another 0.7 mile to Happy Valley, where you can view bright splashes of wildflowers in the summer months.

Miles and Directions

0.0 Enjoy a wonderful view of Tumalo Falls from the viewing platform at the trailhead. Start hiking on the signed North Fork Trail 24.2 as it heads uphill.

0.2	Arrive at a viewpoint of Tumalo Falls.
1.2	Pass a signed viewpoint of Double Falls on the right.
2.2	Pass a signed viewpoint of the Upper Falls on the right. This is your turnaround point. Retrace the same route back to the trailhead.
4.4	Arrive back at the trailhead.

Options

Continue another 2.2 miles to Happy Valley, where you'll find beautiful wildflower scenery during the summer months. Travel 1.5 miles to the intersection with the Swampy Lakes Trail, stay to the right, and continue 0.7 mile to Happy Valley. Or make a loop by traveling 1.5 miles to the intersection with the Swampy Lakes Trail, then turn left and follow

Fall colors are striking in the Tumalo Creek canyon.

the Swampy Lakes Trail for 2.1 miles to the junction with the Bridge Creek Trail. Turn left onto the Bridge Creek Trail and hike 1.3 miles back to the trailhead.

Hike Information

Local Information: Visit Bend, 750 NW Lava Rd., Ste. 160, Bend; (877) 245-8484; visitbend.com

Local Events and Attractions: High Desert Museum, 59800 S. Hwy. 97, Bend; (541) 382-4754; highdesertmuseum.org

Restaurants: Bend Brewing Company, 1019 NW Brooks St., Bend; (541) 383-1599; bendbrewingco.com

Boneyard Brewing, 37 NW Lake Place, Bend; (541) 323-2325; boneyardbeer .com

Crux Fermentation Project, 50 SW Division St., Bend; (541) 385-3333; crux fermentation.com

Deschutes Brewery, 1044 NW Bond St., Bend; (541) 382-9242; deschutesbrewery .com

10 Barrel Brewing, 1135 NW Galveston Ave., Bend; (541) 678-5228; 10barrel .com

Tumalo Falls

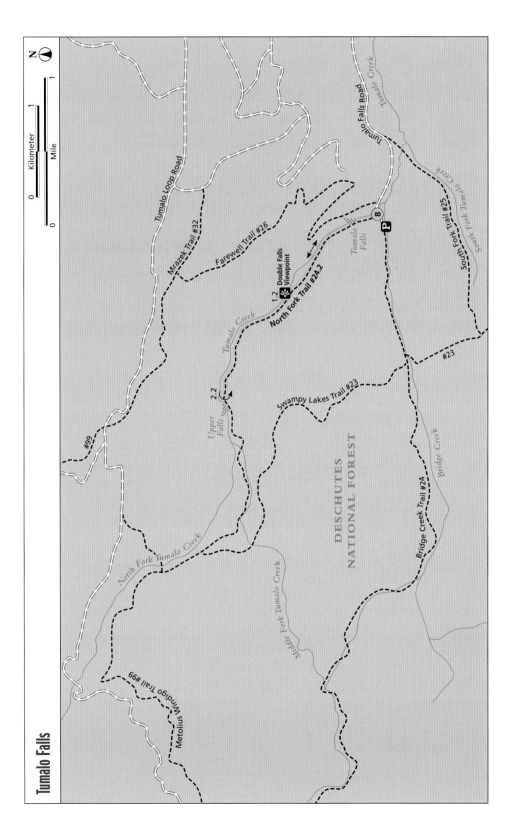

N

Kilometer
0   1

Mile
0   1

Tumalo Loop Road

Mrazek Trail #32

Farewell Trail #26

#99

North Fork Tumalo Creek

Windigo Trail #99

Metolius

Middle Fork Tumalo Creek

Tumalo Creek

Upper Falls

2.2

1.2

Double Falls Viewpoint

North Fork Trail #24.2

Swampy Lakes Trail #23

#23

DESCHUTES NATIONAL FOREST

Bridge Creek Trail #24

Bridge Creek

Tumalo Falls

P

8

Tumalo Falls Road

South Fork Trail #25

South Fork Tumalo Creek

Tumalo Creek

9 Ray Atkeson Memorial Trail

This hike has gorgeous views of Sparks Lake, South Sister, and Broken Top. The trail parallels the edge of the lake and then winds through a thick lodgepole pine forest and past interesting lava flows. You will also have nice views of Mount Bachelor midway through the hike. This hike is a must-do if you crave beautiful lake and mountain views.

Start: Ray Atkeson Memorial Trailhead parking area

Distance: 2.4-mile loop

Hiking time: 1 to 1.5 hours

Difficulty: Easy due to well-graded path and fairly flat terrain

Trail surface: Paved path and dirt path

Best season: Late June through Oct

Other trail users: None

Canine compatibility: Leashed dogs permitted

Land status: Deschutes National Forest

Nearest town: Bend

Fees and permits: A Northwest Forest Pass is required for a small fee. You can purchase a pass at the trailhead, at www.fs.usda.gov/main/deschutes/passes-permits/recreation, or by calling (800) 270-7504.

Schedule: Open all hours

Maps: USGS Broken Top

Trail contact: Deschutes National Forest, Supervisor's Office, 63095 Deschutes Market Rd., Bend; (541) 383-5300; www.fs.usda.gov/main/deschutes/home

Finding the trailhead: From Bend travel 26 miles west on the Cascade Lakes Highway (OR 46) to the turnoff for FR 400 at the Sparks Lake Recreation Area sign. Turn left (south) onto FR 400 and go 0.1 mile to a road junction. Turn left onto FR 100 toward the "Sparks Lake Boat Ramp and Trailheads" sign. Go 1.7 miles and turn left into the Ray Atkeson Memorial Trailhead parking area. GPS: N44 00.791' / W121 44.213'

The Hike

This loop hike takes you past scenic Sparks Lake and through a pine forest with interesting lava outcroppings. The trail is paved and wheelchair accessible for the first 0.4 mile. This hike offers jaw-dropping views of Sparks Lake with South Sister and Broken Top in the background. The trail is named for well-known nature photographer Ray Atkeson. Ray Atkeson was known for his large-format, color scenic photography, and this trail is dedicated to him.

The trail starts by paralleling the shoreline of Sparks Lake, which covers 400 acres and has a depth of 10 feet. Sparks Lake was named for early settler Lige Sparks. The lake is popular with canoeists and kayakers who come here to paddle in the quiet waters, explore the hidden coves, and admire the stunning backdrop of South Sister and Broken Top. After 0.8 mile you have the option to turn left and hike a shorter loop on the signed Davis Canyon Loop Trail.

South Sister is the backdrop for picturesque Sparks Lake.

Halfway through the hike the path leads you up a short hill where you will have more scenic views of Mount Bachelor, South Sister, and Broken Top. The trail continues winding through a lodgepole pine forest until the loop ends at 2.4 miles.

Miles and Directions

0.0   Start hiking on the signed paved trail. Go 100 yards and turn right onto the signed barrier-free trail.

0.2   Enjoy a spectacular view of Sparks Lake, South Sister, and Broken Top.

0.3   Pass a rest bench with more beautiful mountain and lake views.

0.4   The paved path ends.

0.8   Continue straight on the signed hiking loop. (***Option:*** The Davis Canyon Loop Trail goes left at this junction.)

Purple wildflower blooms add splashes of color to the black lava rock that can be seen along this route.

1.4 Arrive at the top of a small knoll that provides a good viewpoint of South Sister, Broken Top, and Mount Bachelor.

1.9 Continue straight (right) at the trail junction (left leads to the trail junction you passed at the 0.8-mile mark).

2.4 The trail turns from dirt to pavement. At the trail junction continue to the right and arrive back at the trailhead in another 100 yards.

Hike Information

Local Information: Visit Bend, 750 NW Lava Rd., Ste. 160, Bend; (877) 245-8484; visitbend.com

Local Events and Attractions: High Desert Museum, 59800 S. Hwy. 97, Bend; (541) 382-4754; highdesertmuseum.org

Restaurants: Bend Brewing Company, 1019 NW Brooks St., Bend; (541) 383-1599; bendbrewingco.com

Ray Atkeson Memorial Trail

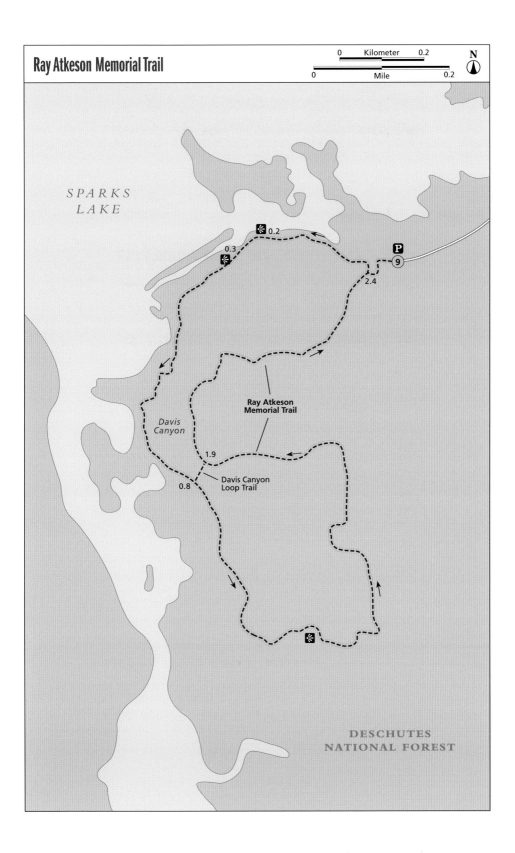

0   Kilometer   0.2

0   Mile   0.2

N

SPARKS LAKE

0.2

0.3

P 9

2.4

Davis Canyon

Ray Atkeson Memorial Trail

1.9

Davis Canyon Loop Trail

0.8

DESCHUTES NATIONAL FOREST

You will have stunning views of South Sister from the Ray Atkeson Memorial Trail.

Crux Fermentation Project, 50 SW Division St., Bend; (541) 385-3333; crux fermentation.com

Deschutes Brewery, 1044 NW Bond St., Bend; (541) 382-9242; deschutesbrewery .com

LODGEPOLE PINE

The lodgepole pine is one of the most prevalent conifer species in the Pacific Northwest and is also one of the most harvested trees. This tree is very tolerant of poor soil and extreme weather conditions. The lodgepole is extremely slow growing and can take almost 100 years to reach 60 feet tall. Its 2-inch-long cones have a layer of resin that seals and protects the cones. During a forest fire the resin is melted and the seeds fall out of the cone. Hundreds of seeds start growing in the ash-enriched soil.

10 Green Lakes

This popular hike parallels enchanting Fall Creek and leads you to the Green Lakes Basin. You can admire this group of high Cascade lakes and also enjoy views of South Sister and Broken Top. A slightly longer loop hike is another option.

Start: Green Lakes Trailhead parking area
Distance: 9.0-mile out-and-back (11.0-mile loop option)
Hiking time: 4 to 6 hours
Difficulty: Difficult due to trail length and elevation gain
Trail surface: Dirt path
Best season: July through Oct
Other trail users: None
Canine compatibility: Leashed dogs permitted
Land status: Deschutes National Forest and Three Sisters Wilderness
Nearest town: Bend
Fees and permits: A Central Cascades Wilderness Permit is required June 15 to Oct 15. Permits must be purchased at Recreation .gov or by calling (877) 444-6777. There are limited permits available due to the popularity of this trail and so it is recommended to purchase your day-use permits ahead of time. Permits are not available at Forest Service offices. If you are hiking at other times during the year a Northwest Forest Pass is required for a small fee. You can purchase a pass at the trailhead, at www.fs.usda.gov/main/ deschutes/passes-permits/recreation, or by calling (800) 270-7504.
Schedule: Open all hours
Maps: USGS Broken Top
Trail contact: Deschutes National Forest, Supervisor's Office, 63095 Deschutes Market Rd., Bend; (541) 383-5300; www.fs.usda.gov/ main/deschutes/home

Finding the trailhead: From the intersection of US 97 (Business) and Franklin Avenue in downtown Bend, turn west onto Franklin Avenue. Proceed 1.2 miles (Franklin Avenue becomes Riverside Boulevard) to the intersection with Tumalo Avenue. Turn right onto Tumalo Avenue (which becomes Galveston Avenue). Go 0.5 mile and turn left onto 14th Street. This street soon becomes Century Drive, also known as the Cascade Lakes Highway (OR 46). Continue about 27 miles on the Cascade Lakes Highway to the Green Lakes Trailhead parking area on the right side of the road. GPS: N44 1.82' /W121 44.152'

The Hike

This popular route takes you on a tour of the Three Sisters Wilderness along the banks of charming Fall Creek. This boulder-strewn creek is filled with beautiful waterfalls around almost every bend. You'll follow the wide, dirt path along the banks of the creek through a fragrant forest. The trail also affords views of the Newberry Lava Flow, which erupted from the southeast side of South Sister— youngest of the Three Sisters volcanoes. Shiny, black obsidian is present in this

Green Lakes at sunset. Photo credit: Ken Skeen.

amazing lava flow. Because of how obsidian is formed (through rapid cooling of lava), it is very hard and extremely sharp. These properties were highly valued by Native Americans, who called the rock *isukws* (pronounced e-shook-wsh) and used it to make arrowheads, knives, jewelry, ornaments, sculptures, ceremonial objects, and tools.

After 4.3 miles you'll enter the magnificent Green Lakes Basin. Three greenish-colored lakes fill the basin. Enjoy the views of the lakes, South Sister, and Broken Top, then return on the same route. If you are feeling ambitious and want to return on the trail via a loop route, follow the Soda Creek Trail 6.3 miles back to the trailhead. See the Miles and Directions section for details. Be sure to arm yourself with mosquito repellent on this hike.

Since this hike is so popular, it is recommended that you hike this trail during the week during July and August if you want to avoid the crowds.

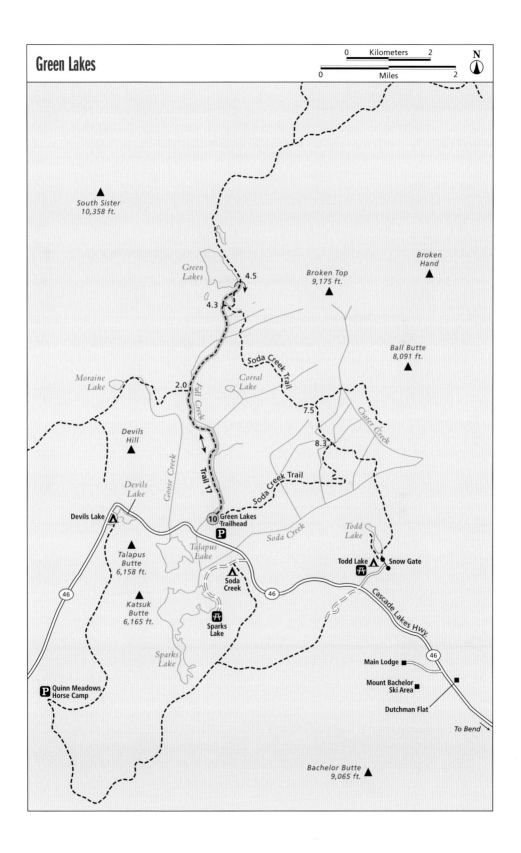

Miles and Directions

0.0 Start hiking on the smooth wide Trail 17, which parallels Fall Creek. A sign at the start of the trail indicates "Moraine Lake 2 Miles/Green Lakes 4.5 Miles/Park Meadow 9 Miles/ Scott Pass 21 Miles." Fall Creek has beautiful waterfalls around almost every bend.

2.0 Arrive at a trail junction. Continue straight (right) on the smooth track as it parallels Fall Creek. (The trail that goes left at this junction heads toward Moraine Lake.)

4.3 Arrive at the Park Meadow/Soda Creek Trail junction. Continue straight to enter the Green Lakes Basin.

4.5 Enjoy views of the lakes and then turn around and return on the same route.

9.0 Arrive back at the Green Lakes Trailhead.

Option

To complete a loop back to the trailhead, you can return on a 6.3-mile route via the Soda Creek Trail.

4.7 Return to the Park Meadow/Soda Creek junction. Walk about 10 yards and then take another quick right turn toward Soda Creek/Broken Top. Continue climbing up the trail, enjoying awesome views of the Green Lakes to the north. The route skirts the south edge of the 9,175-foot Broken Top peak.

7.5 Turn right toward Soda Creek/Todd Lake. (The Broken Top Trail continues left at this junction.)

8.3 Turn right where a sign indicates "Soda Creek." (The trail that goes left heads toward Todd Lake.) From here you'll continue downhill—be ready to negotiate water crossings at Crater and Soda Creeks.

11.0 Arrive back at the Green Lakes Trailhead.

Hike Information

Local Information: Visit Bend, 750 NW Lava Rd., Ste. 160, Bend; (877) 245-8484; visitbend.com

Local Events and Attractions: High Desert Museum, 59800 S. Hwy. 97, Bend; (541) 382-4754; highdesertmuseum.org

Restaurants: Bend Brewing Company, 1019 NW Brooks St., Bend; (541) 383-1599; bendbrewingco.com

Crux Fermentation Project, 50 SW Division St., Bend; (541) 385-3333; cruxfermentation.com

Deschutes Brewery, 1044 NW Bond St., Bend; (541) 382-9242; deschutesbrewery.com

GREEN TIP

Don't take souvenirs home with you. This means natural materials such as plants, rocks, and wildflowers as well as historic artifacts such as fossils and arrowheads.

11 South Sister

The trek up 10,358-foot South Sister, the crown jewel of the Three Sisters Wilderness, is well worth the hard work. The trail starts out by heading through the high, open Wickiup Plain on the way to Lewis Glacier and, finally, the summit crater. At the peak you'll find gorgeous views of Middle and North Sister to the north and Green Lakes, Mount Bachelor, and Broken Top to the southeast. The weather on South Sister is notoriously erratic, so be prepared for anything. If the skies look threatening, don't attempt to reach the summit. Keep in mind that you may find snow on the summit as late as mid-July. If you climb the peak before the snow melts, you'll need waterproof mountaineering boots and an ice ax.

Start: Devils Lake Trailhead off Cascade Lakes Highway

Distance: 11.0-mile out-and-back

Hiking time: 7 to 9 hours

Difficulty: Very difficult due to steep terrain and loose lava scree the last mile of the hike near the summit

Trail surface: Dirt path and loose lava scree

Best season: Late July through Oct

Other trail users: None

Canine compatibility: Leashed dogs permitted. However, it is not recommended to bring dogs on this trail because the sharp lava scree will cut their feet. If you do bring your dog, be sure to bring foot protection for him.

Land status: Three Sisters Wilderness

Nearest town: Bend

Fees and permits: You will need to purchase a limited-entry permit to hike this trail and to park at the trailhead between June 15 and Oct 15. There are 100 day-use permits per day and they are available at www.recreation .gov or by calling (877) 444-6777. If you are hiking at other times during the year a Northwest Forest Pass is required for a small fee. You can purchase a pass at the trailhead, at www.fs.usda.gov/main/deschutes/passes-permits/recreation, or by calling (800) 270-7504. A free self-issue wilderness permit is also required and can be obtained at the trailhead.

Schedule: Open all hours

Maps: USGS South Sister

Trail contact: Deschutes National Forest, Supervisor's Office, 63095 Deschutes Market Rd., Bend; (541) 383-5300; www.fs.usda.gov/main/deschutes/home

Finding the trailhead: From the intersection of US 97 (Business) and Franklin Avenue in downtown Bend, turn west onto Franklin Avenue. Proceed 1.2 miles (Franklin Avenue becomes Riverside Boulevard) to the intersection with Tumalo Avenue. Turn right onto Tumalo Avenue (which becomes Galveston Avenue). Go 0.5 mile and turn left onto 14th Street. This street soon becomes Century Drive, also known as the Cascade Lakes Highway (OR 46). Travel about 28.5 miles west on the Cascade Lakes Highway to the Devils Lake Trailhead, located on the left side of the highway. GPS: N44 2.117' / W121 45.935'

The Hike

The Deschutes National Forest encompasses 1.6 million acres in Central Oregon. The diverse woodland is home to lofty volcanic peaks, interesting lava formations, alpine lakes and forest, and sagebrush- and juniper-covered plateaus and canyons. Some of Oregon's highest peaks are found in this area, including the centerpieces of the 242,400-acre Three Sisters Wilderness: 10,085-foot North Sister, 10,047-foot Middle Sister, and 10,358-foot South Sister. More than 260 miles of trails, including 40 miles of the Pacific Crest Trail, wind through this scenic wilderness area.

Early settlers to the area called the North, Middle, and South Sister Mountains Faith, Hope, and Charity, but these names never gained official recognition. Geologists believe each peak is a separate volcano. Some mountaineers have dubbed the oldest mountain, North Sister, "the Black Beast of the Cascades" because of the difficult route to its summit. The eroding mountain was once a broad shield volcano almost 20 miles wide and 8,000 feet tall. Eruptions added another 3,000 feet, but over the past 300,000 years it has suffered serious erosion. Middle Sister is the second oldest of the three. Though it's the smallest of the three peaks, it has the most symmetrical cone, and situated on the peak's western slope is the impressive Collier Glacier, a 1.5-mile-long ice sheet that has been shrinking for the past hundred years.

Its cone still filled with some ice and snow, South Sister is the baby of the trio. It's thought to date back to the late Pleistocene era. South Sister is also home to Oregon's largest glacier, Prouty, named for climber Harley Prouty, who served as president of the Mazamas, a Portland-based mountaineering group. He was the first person to ascend Prouty Pinnacles on North Sister in August 1910 and is thought to be the first person to reach the summit of North Sister.

It's possible to reach South Sister's summit on a very strenuous out-and-back day hike, but most people like to take it slow and camp along the way at Moraine Lake. Whatever you decide, begin at the Devils Lake Trailhead and start out climbing a steep series of switchbacks through a thick fir forest. After 2 miles you arrive at a junction. If you're climbing to the summit (on a day hike), continue straight. If you're planning to camp for the night, turn right and continue 0.5 mile to Moraine Lake and its twenty-three designated campsites. Watch your step here—the land is very delicate and vulnerable to misuse. Practice zero-impact camping and make every effort to preserve the integrity of the area.

A spur trail leads around the lake and up a canyon and then rejoins the South Sister Trail. Back at the junction (2 miles from the trailhead), continue across the wide-open Wickiup Plain—*wickiup* is the Native American term for a wigwam or tepee. This open alpine landscape is characterized by small islands of trees, long lava ridges, and smooth, glacier-carved basins.

Views of Middle and North Sister are expansive from the summit of South Sister.

At mile 4.4 you'll arrive at the southern tip of Lewis Glacier, named for explorer Meriwether Lewis, who traveled through Oregon in 1805 with his famous partner, William Clark. Stay to the left of the small lake at the base of the glacier and follow a steep and rocky trail to the south rim of South Sister Crater. From there continue 0.2 mile on the Rim Trail to the true summit. Or, if there is still snow in the crater, access the summit by traversing the snowfield.

The scenery at the summit is fantastic. On a clear day, Mount Rainier is visible 180 miles to the north in Washington. There are also inspiring views of the Chambers Lakes and Middle and North Sisters to the north and of Green Lakes, Mount Bachelor, and Broken Top to the southeast. It's often cold and windy at the summit, so bring extra clothing, plenty of food and water, and aspirin if you are prone to altitude sickness.

Miles and Directions

0.0 Start at the Devils Lake Trailhead.

0.1 The trail intersects the Cascade Lakes Highway (OR 46). Cross the highway and continue on the singletrack trail on the other side.

2.0 Continue straight (left) at the trail junction. If you turn right, you'll arrive at Moraine Lake in 0.5 mile. Moraine Lake has designated campsites if you want to stay overnight.

4.4 Arrive at the southern tip of Lewis Glacier. From this point, stay to the left of the glacier on an unofficial trail. The trail is very steep, and as you near the summit, it becomes loose scree.

5.3 Arrive at the south rim of South Sister Crater. Hike another 0.2 mile on the Rim Trail to reach the true summit.

5.5 Reach the true summit of South Sister and your turnaround point. Enjoy views of 10,047-foot Middle Sister, 10,085-foot North Sister, and Chambers Lakes to the north and 9,152-foot Broken Top and Green Lakes to the southeast. Retrace the same route back to the trailhead.

11.0 Arrive back at the Devils Lake Trailhead.

DOGGIE BACKPACKS

Dogs can carry their own gear when they are hiking with you on the trail in their own doggie backpacks. Your dog can carry a load of about 25 percent to 30 percent of his body weight. A dog's age, physical fitness, and frame size are factors that influence how much he can carry. If your dog loves the water, pack food items in waterproof bags in case an irresistible swimming hole appears. You can purchase doggie backpacks at many outdoor retailers such as REI (rei.com) or companies that produce outdoor gear specifically for dogs such as Ruffwear (ruffwear.com).

Hike Information

Local Information: Visit Bend, 750 NW Lava Rd., Ste. 160, Bend; (877) 245-8484; visitbend.com

Local Events and Attractions: High Desert Museum, 59800 S. Hwy. 97, Bend; (541) 382-4754; highdesertmuseum.org

Restaurants: Bend Brewing Company, 1019 NW Brooks St., Bend; (541) 383-1599; bendbrewingco.com

Crux Fermentation Project, 50 SW Division St., Bend; (541) 385-3333; cruxfermentation.com

Deschutes Brewery, 1044 NW Bond St., Bend; (541) 382-9242; deschutesbrewery.com

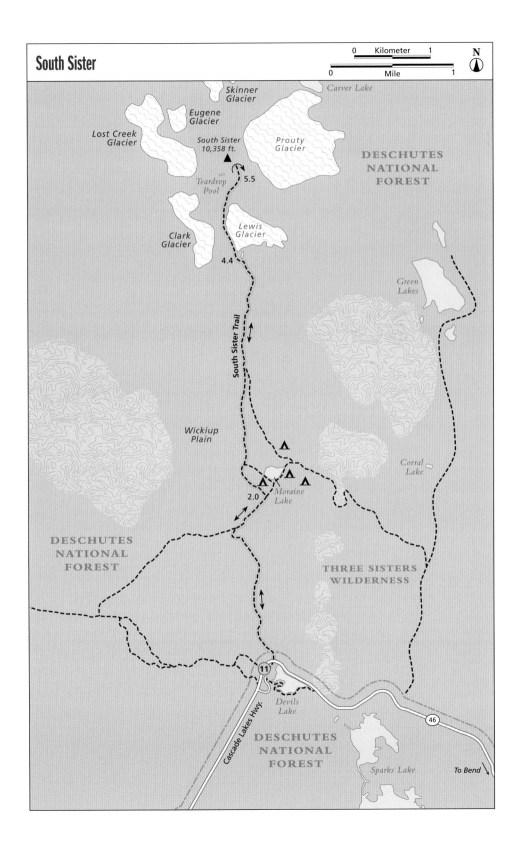

South Sister

0 Kilometer 1
0 Mile 1

N

Skinner Glacier

Eugene Glacier

Lost Creek Glacier

Carver Lake

South Sister 10,358 ft.

Prouty Glacier

DESCHUTES NATIONAL FOREST

Teardrop Pool

5.5

Clark Glacier

Lewis Glacier

4.4

Green Lakes

South Sister Trail

Wickiup Plain

Corral Lake

2.0   Moraine Lake

DESCHUTES NATIONAL FOREST

THREE SISTERS WILDERNESS

11

Cascade Lakes Hwy.

Devils Lake

46

DESCHUTES NATIONAL FOREST

Sparks Lake

To Bend

12 Osprey Point

This route takes you to a spectacular viewpoint of Crane Prairie Reservoir, where you may see ospreys fishing in the productive waters of the reservoir. You also have the option to take a side trip to view the historic Billy Quinn gravesite.

Start: Osprey Point Trailhead off Cascade Lakes Highway

Distance: 0.7-mile lollipop loop

Hiking time: About 1 hour

Difficulty: Easy due to flat terrain and short trail length

Trail surface: Dirt path

Best season: July through Oct

Other trail users: None

Canine compatibility: Dogs permitted

Land status: Deschutes National Forest

Nearest town: Bend

Fees and permits: None

Schedule: Open all hours

Maps: USGS Crane Prairie Reservoir

Trail contact: Deschutes National Forest, Supervisor's Office, 63095 Deschutes Market Rd., Bend; (541) 383-5300; www.fs.usda.gov/main/deschutes/home

Finding the trailhead: From the intersection of US 97 (Business) and Franklin Avenue in downtown Bend, turn west onto Franklin Avenue. Proceed 1.2 miles (Franklin Avenue becomes Riverside Boulevard) to the intersection with Tumalo Avenue. Turn right onto Tumalo Avenue (which becomes Galveston Avenue). Go 0.5 mile and turn left onto 14th Street. This street soon becomes Century Drive, also known as the Cascade Lakes Highway (OR 46). Travel west for about 50 miles on the Cascade Lakes Highway (OR 46) and then south at a turnoff on the left side of the road for the Osprey Point Interpretive Trail. Turn left and continue a short distance to a road fork. Turn left and continue 0.1 mile to a parking area and the trailhead. GPS: N43 46.96' / W121 50.172'

The Hike

This short loop hike gives you the opportunity to look for ospreys hunting and feeding in Crane Prairie Reservoir. The reservoir was originally built in 1920 with private funds. In 1940 the Bureau of Reclamation rebuilt the reservoir to provide irrigation for Central Oregon farmers and ranchers. The dam caused extensive flooding and killed many trees. The dead tree snags provide ideal habitat for nesting ospreys. Related to both hawks and eagles, ospreys are classified in their own family, Pandionidae. These magnificent birds weigh up to 4.5 pounds and have a 6-foot wingspan. They have striking yellow-orange eyes and a predominantly white underside with black markings on the top of their

Ospreys are a common sight on this hike.

wings. Their heads are white with a distinctive black band across the eyes and cheeks. Their plumage is so distinctive and beautiful, it was once used to trim women's hats.

Also known as the fish hawk, the osprey's diet is made up almost entirely of fish. The osprey has the ability to reverse its outer claw, having talons facing both forward and backward so that it can more easily hold on to its catch.

It can also spot fish from as high as 90 feet. Once it spots a good catch, it'll make a fast, arrow-like dive, plunging as far as 4 feet into the water. Ospreys migrate to the high lakes area in early April and lay two to four eggs. The eggs are incubated for 28 to 35 days, and the osprey chicks stay in the nest for up to 10 weeks. In October the adults and young migrate south to Central and South America.

This route weaves through a thick lodgepole pine forest. Listen for squirrels and chipmunks as well as songbirds. At the start of the hike you have the option to walk 0.1 mile to view the Billy Quinn gravesite. Interpretive signs and rest benches invite you to stop and enjoy your surroundings. In late summer, when the water levels are lower, you have the option to hike out into a lush meadow on a primitive trail to the water's edge where you'll have nice views of Mount Bachelor, Broken Top, and the Three Sisters to the north. After enjoying the views, head back to the main loop trail. Finish the loop and retrace the same route back to the trailhead.

Miles and Directions

0.0 Start walking on the Osprey Point Trail 29. (***Option:*** Turn left and walk 0.1 mile to the Billy Quinn gravesite.)

0.3 Arrive at a T junction. Turn right to begin a short loop. From a viewpoint on the loop trail, look for ospreys fishing in the reservoir. (***Option:*** If the water level is low, hike out through a lush meadow to the water's edge.)

0.4 The loop portion of the trail ends. Follow the main trail back to the trailhead.

0.7 Arrive back at the trailhead.

Hike Information

Local Information: Visit Bend, 750 NW Lava Rd., Ste. 160, Bend; (877) 245-8484; visitbend.com

Local Events and Attractions: High Desert Museum, 59800 S. Hwy. 97, Bend; (541) 382-4754; highdesertmuseum.org

Restaurants: Bend Brewing Company, 1019 NW Brooks St., Bend; (541) 383-1599; bendbrewingco.com

Crux Fermentation Project, 50 SW Division St., Bend; (541) 385-3333; cruxfermentation.com

Deschutes Brewery, 1044 NW Bond St., Bend; (541) 382-9242; deschutesbrewery.com

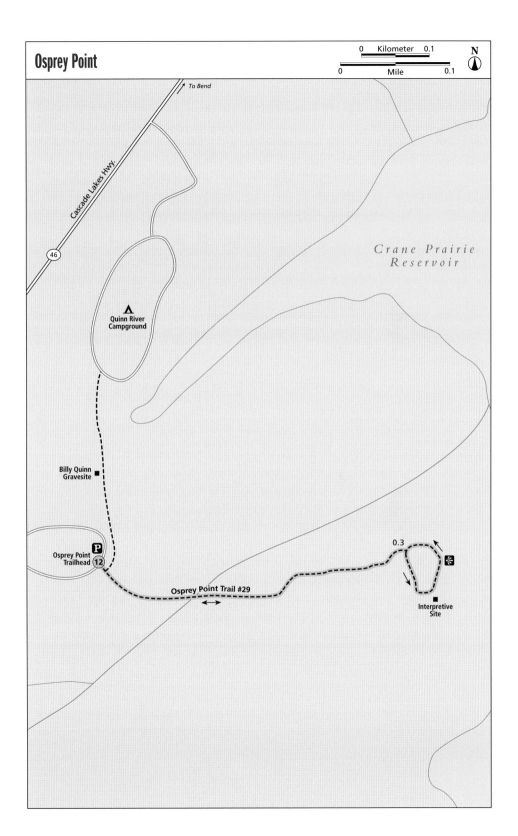

Osprey Point

0   Kilometer   0.1

0   Mile   0.1

N

To Bend

Cascade Lakes Hwy.

46

Crane Prairie Reservoir

Quinn River Campground

Billy Quinn Gravesite

P

Osprey Point Trailhead   12

Osprey Point Trail #29

0.3

Interpretive Site

13 Benham Falls–Deschutes River Trail

This route follows the southern segment of the Deschutes River Trail. It takes you through a magnificent old-growth ponderosa pine forest along the banks of the moody Deschutes River. Highlights of the route include a spectacular viewpoint of Benham Falls, grand views of South Sister and Broken Top, and opportunities to see ospreys and other wildlife. Options to hike farther on the Deschutes River Trail are available.

Start: Benham Falls Day-Use Area
Distance: 2.0-mile out-and-back
Hiking time: 1 to 1.5 hours
Difficulty: Easy due to well-graded trail and flat terrain
Trail surface: Dirt path
Best season: Year-round; snow may be present during the winter months
Other trail users: Trail runners and mountain bikers
Canine compatibility: Leashed dogs permitted
Land status: Deschutes National Forest

Nearest town: Bend
Fees and permits: A Northwest Forest Pass is required for a small fee. You can purchase a pass at www.fs.usda.gov/main/deschutes/passes-permits/recreation or by calling (800) 270-7504.
Schedule: Open all hours
Maps: USGS Benham Falls
Trail contact: Deschutes National Forest, Supervisor's Office, 63095 Deschutes Market Rd., Bend; (541) 383-5300; www.fs.usda.gov/main/deschutes/home

Finding the trailhead: From the intersection of NW Franklin and US 97 in Bend, travel 11.2 miles south on US 97 to a sign that indicates Lava Lands Visitor Center. Turn right (west) onto the entrance road and then take an immediate left onto FR 9702 where a sign reads "Deschutes River 4 / Benham Falls 4." Continue 4 miles to a gravel parking area at the road's end at the Benham Falls Day-Use Area. GPS: N43 54.559' / W121 21.452'

The Hike

This route starts at the picturesque Benham Falls Day-Use Picnic Area that is set among towering old-growth ponderosa pine trees. The day-use area has picnic tables, fire rings, and restrooms. You'll begin the hike by walking on a forested path along the shores of the Deschutes River. The river is very quiet and wide along this section because of a man-made logjam located above the wood bridge that crosses the river. This logjam was built in the 1920s to help protect bridge pilings from debris floating down the river. Plants and grass have grown on top of the logs, creating an "almost" natural dam on the river. At 0.1 mile you'll cross the river over a long wood bridge. Over the next 0.5 mile you'll walk on a wide multiuse path that is popular with mountain bikers. At 0.7 mile you'll turn off the multiuse path onto a hiking trail that follows the contours of the river.

Roaring Benham Falls is one of the highlights of this hike.

As you approach Benham Falls, the character of the river changes from slow and meandering to fast and furious as the river channel narrows. At 0.8 mile you'll arrive at a spectacular viewpoint of Benham Falls. The river roars over jagged lava through a narrow canyon. From here the route continues along the shores of the river, where you'll have views of a magnificent lava flow on the opposite side of the river and spectacular views of South Sister and Broken Top. Ospreys feed and nest along this

The author and her dog Tiz on the Deschutes River.

section of the river. Also known as "fish hawks," they feed on the large stocks of trout present in the river. You can identify ospreys by their predominantly white undersides and black markings on the top of their wings. Their heads are white with a distinctive black band across their eyes and cheeks. Look for their nests, which are usually located in the tops of dead trees.

You have the option to hike farther on the Deschutes River Trail. You can hike another 1.5 miles to Slough Meadow Day-Use Area, or you can continue another 7.7 miles to the Meadow Picnic Area. If you want to hike one way, you can set up

Benham Falls–Deschutes River Trail

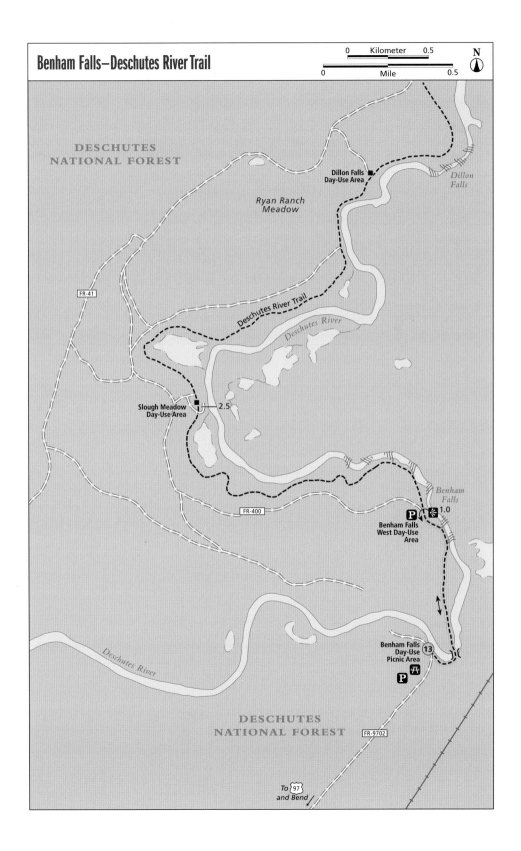

0   Kilometer   0.5

0   Mile   0.5

N

DESCHUTES
NATIONAL FOREST

Ryan Ranch
Meadow

Dillon Falls
Day-Use Area

Dillon
Falls

FR-41

Deschutes River Trail

Deschutes River

Slough Meadow
Day-Use Area

2.5

FR-400

Benham
Falls

1.0

P

Benham Falls
West Day-Use
Area

Deschutes River

Benham Falls
Day-Use
Picnic Area

13

P

DESCHUTES
NATIONAL FOREST

FR-9702

To 97
and Bend

a shuttle by leaving a vehicle at the Meadow Day-Use Area. See below for driving directions to the Meadow Day-Use Area.

Miles and Directions

0.0   Start by hiking on the trail signed "Deschutes River Trail No. 2.1," which begins at the river's edge opposite the picnic area. Another sign indicates "Benham Falls ½, Dillon Falls 3½, Lava Island Falls 7, Meadow Day Use 8½."

0.1   Cross a long wood bridge over the Deschutes River.

0.7   Veer right onto the hiking trail, indicated by a hiker symbol.

0.8   The hiking trail intersects the wide biking trail. Turn right and continue on the narrower hiking trail. Proceed about 200 yards to a T intersection. Turn right and descend to a viewpoint of Benham Falls. (If you go left at this junction, you'll arrive at the Benham Falls West Day-Use Area, which has restrooms and picnic tables.)

1.0   Arrive at a scenic viewpoint of Benham Falls. After enjoying the view, turn around and head back uphill to the trail junction. Retrace the same route back to the trailhead.

2.0   Arrive back at the trailhead.

Options

You can hike another 1.5 miles on the Deschutes River Trail to Slough Meadow, or if you are looking for an all-day hike, you can continue another 7.7 miles to the Meadow Day-Use Area. Leave a second vehicle at the Meadow Day-Use Area for a one-way shuttle option. Travel 6.2 miles west of Bend on the Cascade Lakes Highway (OR 46) and turn left onto gravel FR 100 at the Meadow Picnic Area sign. Continue 1.4 miles to the parking area and trailhead.

Hike Information

Local Information: Visit Bend, 750 NW Lava Rd., Ste. 160, Bend; (877) 245-8484; visitbend.com

Local Events and Attractions: Sunriver Nature Center, 57245 River Rd., Sunriver; (541) 593-4394; snco.org

High Desert Museum, 59800 S. Hwy. 97, Bend; (541) 382-4754; highdesert museum.org

BALD EAGLES

The bald eagle is the largest bird of prey in the Northwest and is easy to identify with its white head and tail feathers. Young bald eagles do not obtain the white head and tail feathers until 5 to 7 years of age. The female bald eagle is larger than the male and weighs 10 to 15 pounds, has a wingspan of almost 8 feet, and is up to 3 feet tall. They build their nests in broken treetops, often near bodies of water. They feed on fish, wounded waterfowl, and the carcasses of winter-killed deer or elk.

14 Lava Lands Visitor Center Trails

This route combines two trails: the Trail of the Molten Land and the Trail of the Whispering Pines, which are both accessed from the Lava Lands Visitor Center. The first trail takes you on a journey through an amazing lava flow to a viewpoint with spectacular views of the Central Cascade Mountains. The second trail winds through a second-growth ponderosa forest and has interpretive signs explaining the plants, animals, and history of the area.

Start: Lava Lands Visitor Center
Distance: 1.4-mile figure eight
Hiking time: 30 minutes to 1 hour
Difficulty: Easy due to smooth trail surface and minimal elevation gain
Trail surface: Dirt trail and paved path
Best season: May through Oct
Other trail users: None
Canine compatibility: Leashed dogs permitted
Land status: National monument
Nearest town: Bend

Fees and permits: A Northwest Forest Pass is required for a small fee. You can purchase a pass at the entrance booth, at www.fs.usda.gov/main/deschutes/passes-permits/recreation, or by calling (800) 270-7504.
Schedule: Dawn to dusk
Maps: USGS Lava Butte
Trail contact: Lava Lands Visitor Center, 58201 S. Hwy. 97, Bend; (541) 593-2421; www.fs.usda.gov/main/deschutes/home
Other: Visitor center open 9 a.m. to 5 p.m. daily May through Sept 30

Finding the trailhead: From the intersection of NW Franklin and US 97 in Bend, travel 11.2 miles south on US 97 to the Lava Lands Visitor Center located on the right and park in the main parking area. GPS: N43 54.591' / W121 21.412'

The Hike

This short hike takes you on a tour of the moonlike landscape of a spectacular lava flow—the result of the eruption of Lava Butte that occurred between 6,000 and 7,000 years ago. When Lava Butte erupted, the lava flowed in three main channels, covering 10 square miles and blocking the Deschutes River in five different locations.

The hike begins adjacent to the Lava Lands Visitor Center (open 9 a.m. to 5 p.m. daily May through the end of September), which is filled with exhibits on the area's geology, animals, and plants. A small selection of maps and books is also available. You'll follow the Trail of the Molten Land as it winds through the lava flow. Interpretive signs help identify important features about the lava flow, including surface tubes and lava channels. The basalt that surrounds you on this trail is not

This route travels through a jumbled lava flow with scenic Lava Butte as a backdrop.

Lava Butte.

as shiny and brilliant as obsidian because it does not contain as much silica (glass), leaving it with a duller appearance. Lava Butte rises sharply from the lava field and is a major landmark on this hike. Lava Butte was created from gas-charged basalt rocks called cinders that were part of a large lava eruption. As these cinders cooled, they formed the butte.

After 0.7 mile you'll arrive at the Phil Brogan Viewpoint. From this high viewpoint you'll have far-reaching views of the immense lava flow and the Central Cascade Mountains. From here you'll complete the short Trail of the Molten Land loop and then continue walking on the Trail of the Whispering Pines. This short interpretive trail weaves through a second-growth forest of ponderosa and lodgepole pines. Interpretive signs describe some of the native plants that grow here, including snowbrush, manzanita, and squaw currant. Native Americans used these plants in a variety of ways. The bark and roots of the snowbrush plant were used as an astringent, manzanita seeds were ground into flower, and parts of the squaw currant were used to cure stomach ailments.

Miles and Directions

0.0 From the main parking area, start walking on a paved path toward the visitor center. (You'll reach a trail junction before you reach the visitor center.) Turn left onto the paved path. Continue about another 50 feet to another trail junction and turn right. (The Trail of the Whispering Pines goes left at this junction.) At the next trail junction, continue straight on the signed Trail of the Molten Land.

0.3 Turn left at the trail junction.

0.5 Turn left toward the signed Phil Brogan Viewpoint.

0.7 Arrive at the Phil Brogan Viewpoint. Take a break on the wood benches and soak in the view of the Central Cascade Mountains and the magnificent lava flow. Walk down the viewpoint trail to the junction with the Trail of the Molten Land Trail and turn left.

1.0 The loop portion of the trail ends. Continue straight (left).

1.2 Turn right at the trail junction toward the signed Trail of the Whispering Pines.

1.3 Turn right and continue on the paved Trail of the Whispering Pines.

1.4 The Trail of the Whispering Pines ends at the parking area and your starting point.

Hike Information

Local Information: Visit Bend, 750 NW Lava Rd., Ste. 160, Bend; (877) 245-8484; visitbend.com

Local Events and Attractions: High Desert Museum, 59800 S. Hwy. 97, Bend; (541) 382-4754; highdesertmuseum.org

Sunriver Nature Center, 57245 River Rd., Sunriver; (541) 593-4394; snco.org

GREEN TIP
When choosing trail snacks, go with homemade
goodies that aren't packaged.

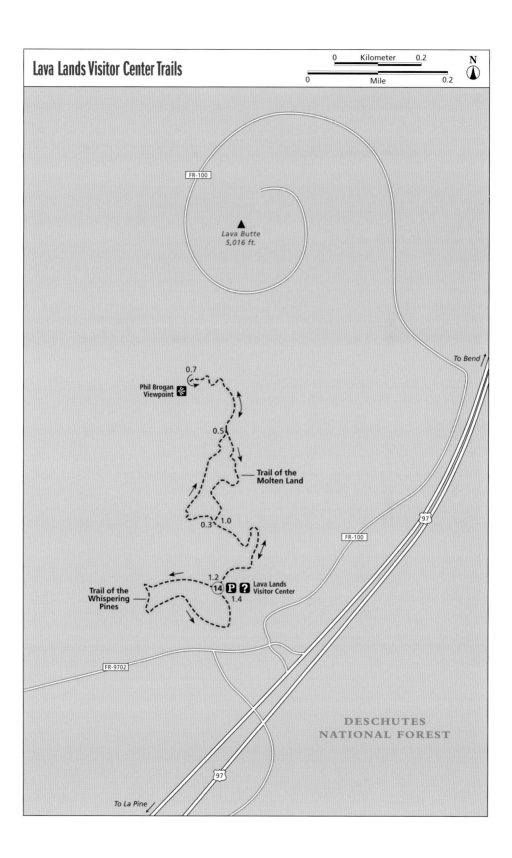

Lava Lands Visitor Center Trails

0 Kilometer 0.2

0 Mile 0.2

N

FR-100

▲
Lava Butte
5,016 ft.

To Bend

0.7

Phil Brogan
Viewpoint

0.5

Trail of the
Molten Land

0.3 1.0

1.2

1.4

14 P ? Lava Lands
Visitor Center

Trail of the
Whispering
Pines

FR-100

97

FR-9702

DESCHUTES
NATIONAL FOREST

97

To La Pine

15 Fall River

This beautiful trail follows the course of the spring-fed Fall River. The uncrowded route takes you through immense groves of ponderosa pine trees and offers many scenic viewpoints of the river, where you may see Canada geese, ospreys, and mallard ducks.

Start: Parking area on FR 42, 0.7 mile past Fall River Campground
Distance: 6.4-mile out-and-back
Hiking time: 2.5 to 3.5 hours
Difficulty: Easy due to smooth, flat trail surface
Trail surface: Dirt path and doubletrack road
Best season: June through Oct
Other trail users: None
Canine compatibility: Dogs permitted

Land status: Deschutes National Forest
Nearest town: Bend
Fees and permits: None
Schedule: Open all hours
Maps: USGS Pistol Butte
Trail contact: Deschutes National Forest, Supervisor's Office, 63095 Deschutes Market Rd., Bend; (541) 383-5300; www.fs.usda.gov/main/deschutes/home

Finding the trailhead: From the intersection of Greenwood Avenue and US 97 (Business) in Bend, travel 16.7 miles south on US 97. Turn right (west) onto Vandevert Road at the Vandevert Road/Fall River sign. Continue for 1 mile to the junction with South Century Drive. Turn left and go 1 mile to the junction with Cascade Lakes Highway (FR 42). Turn right and continue 10.4 miles (you'll pass Fall River Campground on the left after 9.7 miles) to a circular parking area on the left side of the road. GPS: N43 46.120' / W121 38.006'

The Hike

Located in the Deschutes National Forest southwest of Bend, Fall River is a beautiful spring-fed river stocked with brown, brook, and rainbow trout. The source of the river is situated about 2 miles northwest of Pringle Falls on the Deschutes River. From this location the river meanders northeast for about 8 miles until it joins the Deschutes River about 6 miles below Pringle Falls.

This route parallels the course of the river for 3.2 miles. The tour takes you through a forest corridor of stately ponderosa pine trees. These yellow-barked giants are prized for their clear, even grain, which is used for door and window frames. This hardy tree is fire resistant and survives drought better than any other Northwest tree. The root system is deep and extensively branched, and the tree can survive on only 8 to 12 inches of rain per year. These amazing trees can live to be 400 to 500 years of age and grow to be more than 120 feet tall and 5 feet in diameter.

After 0.7 mile you'll arrive at quiet Fall River Campground. This Forest Service campground has twelve tent sites with picnic tables, fire grills, and vault toilets.

Hikers enjoying the view of Fall River.

You'll hike through the campground for 0.1 mile and then continue on the single-track trail next to campsite #8. From here the forest deepens, with thick stands of lodgepole pines. These trees are also drought and fire resistant and have the ability to live in poor soils. They grow very slowly, and it may take a century for a tree to

You will find a lot of solitude on the Fall River Hike.

reach a height of 60 feet. Native Americans used the long, thin trunks of these trees as supporting poles for their tepee lodges.

As the trail approaches the river's edge, watch for Canada geese and ducks feeding in the water. Also be on the lookout for ospreys perched in the dead tree snags along the river's edge. After 1.2 miles you'll walk on a doubletrack road for 0.4 mile and then turn back onto a singletrack trail until the trail's end and your turnaround point at 3.2 miles.

Fall River

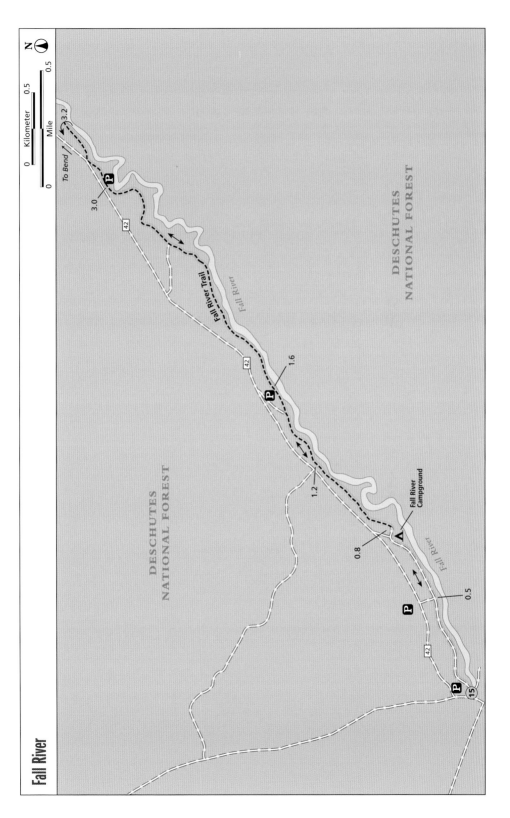

N

0   Kilometer   0.5

0   Mile   0.5

To Bend

3.2

3.0

P

42

Fall River Trail

42

Fall River

1.6

P

1.2

DESCHUTES
NATIONAL FOREST

0.8

Fall River
Campground

P

0.5

Fall River

42

P

15

DESCHUTES
NATIONAL FOREST

A picturesque bridge over Fall River.

Miles and Directions

0.0 From the parking area, look to your left and begin hiking on the doubletrack road that begins adjacent to the wood pole fence. Go 75 yards and then veer left onto a smaller doubletrack road. This road soon becomes a singletrack trail that takes you through a corridor of large ponderosa pine trees.

0.5 Arrive at a sign (facing the other way) that states "End of Trail/Parking on Road 42." Ignore the sign and continue heading east on the trail as it parallels the Fall River.

0.6 Turn right at the brown hiker sign.

0.7 Arrive at Fall River Campground Day-Use Area. (Restrooms are available on your left.) Turn onto the campground loop road and continue hiking through the campground.

0.8 Turn right onto the unsigned Fall River Trail that begins just to the left of campsite #8 and takes you through a thick lodgepole pine forest near the river's edge.

1.2 The trail intersects a red-cinder road. Turn right onto the cinder road.

1.5 Turn right onto an unsigned doubletrack road.

1.6 Turn right onto an unsigned singletrack trail.

3.0 Walk straight across a parking area and continue hiking on the signed Fall River Trail.

3.2 Arrive at a rock dam across the river and an "End of Trail" sign. This is your turnaround point. Retrace the same route back to your starting point.

6.4 Arrive back at the parking area.

Hike Information

Local Information: Visit Bend, 750 NW Lava Rd., Ste. 160, Bend; (877) 245-8484; visitbend.com

Local Events and Attractions: High Desert Museum, 59800 S. Hwy. 97, Bend; (541) 382-4754; highdesertmuseum.org

Sunriver Nature Center, 57245 River Rd., Sunriver; (541) 593-4394; snco.org

16 Big Obsidian Flow Trail

The Big Obsidian Flow Trail is an easy and convenient way to check out Oregon's youngest lava flow. Located in Newberry National Volcanic Monument, this fascinating path crosses the lava flow and highlights the volcanic history of the area. Interpretive signs along the way explain how Native Americans visited the area to collect obsidian for making jewelry and tools.

Start: Big Obsidian Trailhead off Paulina Lake Road (FR 21)
Distance: 0.7-mile loop
Hiking time: 30 minutes to 1 hour
Difficulty: Easy due to minimal elevation gain
Trail surface: Dirt path and stairs
Best season: June through Oct
Other trail users: None
Canine compatibility: Leashed dogs permitted
Land status: National monument

Nearest town: Bend
Fees and permits: National monument entrance fee required
Schedule: Dawn to dusk
Maps: USGS East Lake
Trail contact: Deschutes National Forest, Supervisor's Office, 63095 Deschutes Market Rd., Bend; (541) 383-5300; www.fs.usda.gov/main/deschutes/home

Finding the trailhead: From the intersection of Greenwood Avenue and US 97 in Bend, travel south on US 97 for 23 miles to a sign for Newberry National Volcanic Monument and Paulina and East Lakes. Turn left onto Paulina Lake Road (FR 21) and drive 15.4 miles to the Big Obsidian Trailhead parking area on the right side of the road. GPS: N43 42.388' / W121 14.152'

The Hike

One of the main attractions at the 50,000-acre Newberry National Volcanic Monument is the Big Obsidian Flow Trail, which provides a fascinating tour of Oregon's youngest lava flow. The trail, which begins as a flat, paved path, offers panoramic views of the flow and includes interpretive signs intended to make understanding the landscape easy. The lava rock is very sharp, so be sure to wear sturdy shoes.

After a short distance the path ascends a steep set of metal stairs and, at the top, arrives at the flow itself, a vast spread of gray pumice interspersed with shiny glass-like boulders of obsidian. Just past the stairs the trail comes to a T intersection. From here you can go right or left to begin a 0.3-mile loop. The loop offers outstanding views of 7,984-foot Paulina Peak and the Paulina and East Lakes, located at the center of 17-square-mile Newberry Crater.

The 1,300-year-old flow, which covers 1.1 square miles and has an average thickness of 150 feet, began as extremely hot magma (up to 1,600 degrees Fahrenheit) trapped by the earth's crust 2 to 4 miles underground. The magma eventually found weak points in the earth's surface, and a violent eruption ensued. Later, as the eruption slowed, the sticky magma began oozing out of the earth and crawling over the landscape.

Hikers walking through the moonlike landscape on the Big Obsidian Flow.

One of the more interesting features of the present-day rough and jumbled flow is the glass-like obsidian found on its surface. Due to the way obsidian is formed (through rapid cooling of the lava), it is very hard and extremely sharp. These properties were highly valued by Native Americans, who called the rock *isukws* (pronounced e-shook-wsh). They made arrowheads, knives, jewelry, ornaments, sculptures, ceremonial objects, and tools out of the obsidian to trade with other tribes for fish, shells, and roots. Artifacts dating back 10,000 years have been found in the monument and surrounding areas. You can read about these relics of the past as you walk the trail.

Miles and Directions

0.0 Start hiking on the paved path by the parking area.
0.1 Ascend a set of metal stairs to the lava flow.
0.2 Turn right to begin the loop portion of the trail.
0.5 Turn right (this is the end of the loop).
0.7 Arrive back at the parking area.

Hike Information

Local Information: Visit Bend, 750 NW Lava Rd., Ste. 160, Bend; (877) 245-8484; visitbend.com
Local Events and Attractions: High Desert Museum, 59800 S. Hwy. 97, Bend; (541) 382-4754; highdesertmuseum.org
Sunriver Nature Center, 57245 River Rd., Sunriver; (541) 593-4394; snco.org

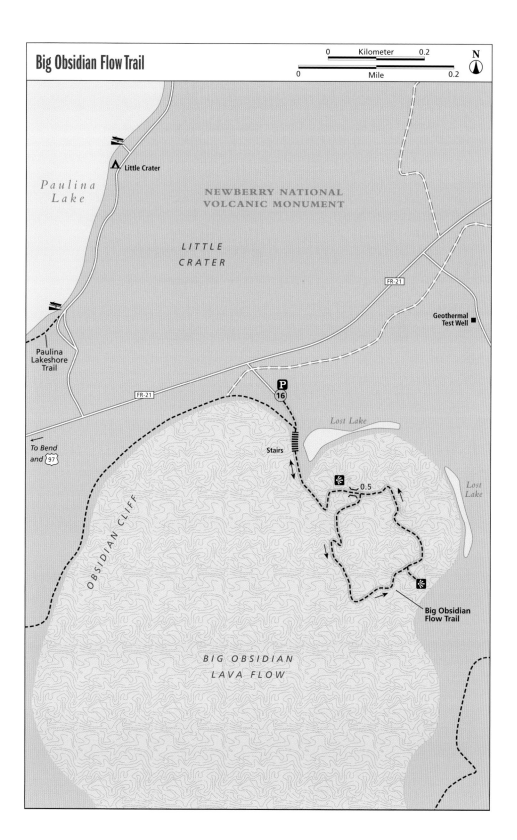

Big Obsidian Flow Trail

0   Kilometer   0.2

0   Mile   0.2

N

Paulina Lake

Little Crater

NEWBERRY NATIONAL
VOLCANIC MONUMENT

*LITTLE
CRATER*

FR-21

Geothermal
Test Well

Paulina
Lakeshore
Trail

FR-21

P
16

To Bend
and 97

Stairs

Lost Lake

0.5

Lost
Lake

OBSIDIAN CLIFF

Big Obsidian
Flow Trail

*BIG OBSIDIAN
LAVA FLOW*

17 Paulina Peak

This route takes you to the summit of Paulina Peak. From the summit you'll have gorgeous views of Paulina and East Lakes, Newberry Caldera, and the Big Obsidian Lava Flow.

Start: Paulina Peak Trailhead off Paulina Lake Road (FR 21)
Distance: 6.0-mile out-and-back
Hiking time: 3.5 to 4.5 hours
Difficulty: Difficult due to steep elevation gain and length of route
Trail surface: Dirt path
Best season: July through Oct
Other trail users: None
Canine compatibility: Leashed dogs permitted

Land status: National monument
Nearest town: Bend
Fees and permits: National monument entrance fee required
Schedule: Dawn to dusk
Maps: USGS Paulina Peak
Trail contact: Deschutes National Forest, Supervisor's Office, 63095 Deschutes Market Rd., Bend; (541) 383-5300; www.fs.usda.gov/main/deschutes/home

Finding the trailhead: From the intersection of Greenwood Avenue and US 97 in Bend, travel south on US 97 for 23 miles to a sign for Newberry National Volcanic Monument and Paulina and East Lakes. Turn left onto Paulina Lake Road (FR 21) and drive 13.2 miles to the visitor center. The trailhead is 50 feet before the visitor center on the right side of the road. GPS: N43 42.694' / W121 16.620'

The Hike

Established in 1990, the 50,000-acre Newberry National Volcanic Monument showcases Newberry Caldera, a 17-square-mile volcanic crater. This area is absolutely teeming with geologic history. You'll find hot springs, lava flows, and cinder cones, all of which can be explored on well-established trails.

One particularly noteworthy trail is the 3-mile path to the summit of 7,984-foot Paulina Peak, the highest point in the monument. The trail begins just to the right of the visitor center in a lodgepole pine forest—the straight and slender lodgepole pines grow in thick stands and are distinguished by their prickly cones and pairs of 2-inch-long needles. After 0.5 mile over fairly flat terrain, the path begins a steep climb. The higher it gets, the better the views become, and soon you'll see Paulina and East Lakes below. At the summit you'll find restrooms, a parking area, and a signed viewpoint. A road leads to the summit, and so you will be sharing the view with others who have driven to the summit.

Enjoy spectacular views of Paulina and East Lakes from the Paulina Peak summit. Note the Big Obsidian Lava Flow on the right that reaches toward Paulina Lake.

Rising prominently from Paulina Lake, Paulina Peak offers spectacular views of the mountains and high desert country of Central Oregon. The peak is what remains of ancient Mount Newberry, which, at 10,000 feet above sea level, was once the highest volcano in the Paulina Mountains. About 200,000 years ago, Newberry erupted and collapsed. The huge caldera left in its place eventually filled with water to create an enormous lake. Thousands of years later, more eruptions split the water into two separate lakes (Paulina and East) and left a central cone and several obsidian flows. The most recent eruption, which occurred about 1,300 years ago, resulted in the Big Obsidian Lava Flow visible to the east.

Before you trek to the top of Paulina Peak, stop in at the visitor center near the trailhead. There you'll find informative brochures (including advice on what to do about bears), information on camping, and ideas on other things to see and do while in the monument.

Miles and Directions

0.0 Start at the Paulina Peak Trailhead sign, located approximately 50 feet to the right of the visitor center. The sign reads "Crater Rim Trail #57/Paulina Peak 3 Miles."
1.5 Enjoy nice views of Paulina and East Lakes.
2.7 Continue straight toward Paulina Peak. (***Option:*** If you go right, you'll intersect FR 500 in 0.5 mile on Trail 58.)
3.0 Arrive at the top of Paulina Peak. This is your turnaround point. There are restrooms and a signed viewpoint located here. Retrace the same route back to the trailhead.
6.0 Arrive back at the trailhead.

Hike Information

Local Information: Visit Bend, 750 NW Lava Rd., Ste. 160, Bend; (877) 245-8484; visitbend.com

Local Events and Attractions: High Desert Museum, 59800 S. Hwy. 97, Bend; (541) 382-4754; highdesertmuseum.org

Sunriver Nature Center, 57245 River Rd., Sunriver; (541) 593-4394; snco.org

GREEN TIP
Be courteous of others. Many people visit natural areas for quiet, peace, and solitude, so avoid making loud noises and intruding on others' privacy.

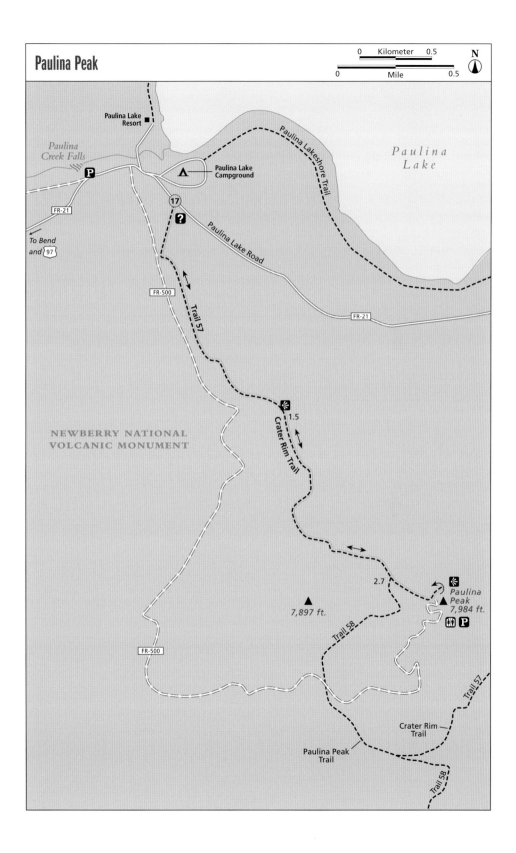

Paulina Peak

0   Kilometer   0.5

0   Mile   0.5

N

Paulina Lake Resort

Paulina Creek Falls

P

FR-21

To Bend and 97

17

?

Paulina Lake Campground

Paulina Lakeshore Trail

Paulina Lake

Paulina Lake Road

FR-21

FR-500

Trail 57

Crater Rim Trail

1.5

NEWBERRY NATIONAL
VOLCANIC MONUMENT

2.7

▲
7,897 ft.

Paulina Peak
7,984 ft.
P

Trail 58

FR-500

Trail 57

Crater Rim Trail

Paulina Peak Trail

Trail 58

18 Paulina Lakeshore Loop

This scenic hike follows the Paulina lakeshore in the Newberry National Volcanic Monument.

Start: Paulina Lakeshore Trailhead off Paulina Lake Road (FR 21)
Distance: 7.5-mile loop
Hiking time: 3 to 4 hours
Difficulty: Moderate due to changes in trail surface and length of route
Trail surface: Dirt path
Best season: July through Oct
Other trail users: None
Canine compatibility: Leashed dogs permitted

Land status: National monument
Nearest town: Bend
Fees and permits: National monument entrance fee required
Schedule: Dawn to dusk
Maps: USGS Paulina Lake
Trail contact: Deschutes National Forest, Supervisor's Office, 63095 Deschutes Market Rd., Bend; (541) 383-5300; www.fs.usda.gov/main/deschutes/home

Finding the trailhead: From the intersection of Greenwood Avenue and US 97 in Bend, travel south on US 97 for 23 miles to a sign for Newberry National Volcanic Monument and Paulina and East Lakes. Turn left onto Paulina Lake Road (FR 21) and travel 11.6 miles to the entrance booth on the left. Continue 1.6 miles past the entrance booth to the Paulina Lakeshore Trailhead on the left. GPS: N43 42.736' / W121 16.565'

The Hike

The loop hike around Paulina Lake is located in the 50,000-acre Newberry National Volcanic Monument, a national preserve that was established in 1990. At the heart of this national monument is the 17-square-mile Newberry Caldera crater, which houses Paulina and East Lakes. Paulina Lake (250 feet deep) and East Lake (180 feet deep) were a single very large lake until lava flows split them apart approximately 6,200 years ago. Today these two lakes are designated as a wildlife refuge supporting bald eagles, ducks, geese, ospreys, and tundra swans. Mammals roaming the shores and surrounding peaks and valleys include badgers, black bears, deer, elk, and pine martens. These lakes are also popular with anglers, and you'll most likely see them fishing for rainbow trout, brown trout, and blackwater trout. The blackwater trout were introduced to the lake to help control the populations of tui chub fish that have reproduced rapidly in Paulina and East Lakes and threaten the quality of the trout catch in both lakes. Blackwater trout are very aggressive and feed on the tui chub; it is hoped they will help reduce this species of fish in the lakes.

Newberry Volcano is located along a group of faults called the Northwest Rift Zone and is one of the largest shield volcanoes in the United States. Shield volcanoes are formed mainly by fluid lava flows pouring from a central vent to form a broad,

Paulina Lakeshore Loop.

gently sloping, dome-shaped cone. The volcano's most recent activity occurred 1,300 years ago, when it deposited more than 170 million cubic yards of obsidian and pumice into what is now called Big Obsidian Lava Flow.

This fun hike circles Paulina Lake. The route takes you past prime swimming beaches, hot springs (located in the northeast section of the lake), and areas filled with shiny black obsidian and stellar views of 7,984-foot Paulina Peak. Be prepared for cool weather and bring plenty of mosquito repellent.

Miles and Directions

0.0   From the paved parking area, start hiking around the lake in a counterclockwise direction on the signed Paulina Lakeshore Trail. The trail starts out as a gravel path lined with stones.

0.1   Walk across a paved boat ramp and then continue walking on the signed trail. Not far past this junction, a sign indicates "Little Crater Campground 2.5 Miles."

2.2   Arrive at a paved boat ramp that has a restroom and picnic tables. After crossing the paved boat ramp, you'll arrive at a sign that states "Paulina Lakeshore Loop Trail/Trail Follows Road." From this point, follow the paved road as it parallels the lakeshore.

2.4   Arrive at the entrance to Little Crater Campground. Continue on the paved road through the campground as it follows the lakeshore.

2.5   Pass a restroom and water faucet. Follow the road through the campground until it ends. Turn right into a gravel trailhead parking lot and continue walking on the Paulina Lakeshore Trail. Take the trail that goes left.

4.0   Turn right at the trail sign.

6.9   Pass several vacation cabins on your right. The trail becomes faint here; keep following the lakeshore.

7.0   Turn right onto a gravel road next to the Paulina Lake Resort general store.

7.1   The road turns to pavement.

7.2   Turn left onto the unsigned dirt singletrack trail.

7.3   Turn left onto a paved road and then cross a concrete bridge over Paulina Creek. Immediately after crossing the bridge, turn left and go down a set of stone steps and then continue on the unsigned dirt trail.

7.5   Arrive back at the trailhead.

Hike Information

Local Information: Visit Bend, 750 NW Lava Rd., Ste. 160, Bend; (877) 245-8484; visitbend.com

Local Events and Attractions: High Desert Museum, 59800 S. Hwy. 97, Bend; (541) 382-4754; highdesertmuseum.org

Sunriver Nature Center, 57245 River Rd., Sunriver; (541) 593-4394; snco.org

SISTERS

Located about 20 miles northwest of Bend, Sisters is a fun Western-themed town filled with many unique shops, galleries, and restaurants. The town's name was inspired by the Three Sisters Mountains—known to early settlers as Faith, Hope, and Charity—which rise impressively from the pine-filled valley surrounding Sisters. Before 1900 Sisters was the only settlement between Prineville and the Cascade Mountains and was an important stopping point for people traveling through the state. It was also the local supply center for farmers and ranchers. In the early 1900s the town began to grow and soon hosted a sawmill, hotel, saloon, blacksmith shop, real estate office, schoolhouse, and mercantile store.

Sisters is a major access point to the Deschutes National Forest, the Mount Washington Wilderness, and the Three Sisters Wilderness. If you want to explore hikes next to scenic creeks and rivers, try the Whychus Creek Trail, Whychus Canyon Preserve, or the West Metolius River Trail. If you are in the mood for gorgeous mountain scenery, hike to the top of Black Crater, Black Butte, or Tam McArthur Rim. To see close-up views of lava flows, try the Little Belknap Crater or the Lava River Trail—Dee Wright Observatory hikes. If you want to see gorgeous mountain scenery from a high alpine meadow, try the Canyon Creek Meadows hike. To visit some high alpine lakes, check out the Hand Lake hike and the Matthieu Lakes Loop hike.

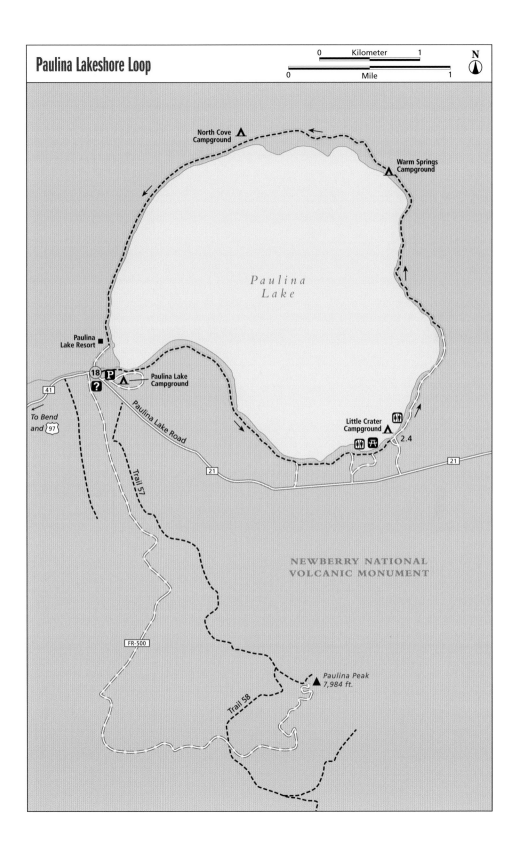

Paulina Lakeshore Loop

0   Kilometer   1

0   Mile   1

N

North Cove
Campground

Warm Springs
Campground

*Paulina
Lake*

Paulina
Lake Resort

18   P

41

Paulina Lake
Campground

Little Crater
Campground

2.4

To Bend
and 97

Paulina Lake Road

Trail 57

21

21

FR-500

NEWBERRY NATIONAL
VOLCANIC MONUMENT

Trail 58

▲ Paulina Peak
7,984 ft.

19 West Metolius River Trail

This unique trail traces the banks of the clear, fast-moving Metolius River and meanders through a lush riparian ecosystem of bright wildflowers and riverside vegetation. The spring-fed river rushes over lava to create swirling rapids and big eddies that are home to various species of salmon and trout. At the turnaround point is the Wizard Falls Fish Hatchery, a great place to take a break and explore. Water and restrooms are available at the fish hatchery. Trails continue to follow the river north on both sides for longer hike options.

Start: Trailhead at road's end in Lower Canyon Creek Campground
Distance: 5.0-mile out-and-back
Hiking time: 2 to 3 hours
Difficulty: Easy due to well-graded path and fairly flat terrain
Trail surface: Dirt path
Best season: Year-round; snow may be present during the winter months
Other trail users: None
Canine compatibility: Leashed dogs permitted

Land status: Deschutes National Forest
Nearest town: Sisters
Fees and permits: None
Schedule: Open all hours
Maps: USGS Black Butte, Candle Creek, and Prairie Farm Spring
Trail contact: Deschutes National Forest, Sisters Ranger District, 201 N. Pine St. and Hwy. 20, Sisters; (541) 549-7700, www.fs.usda.gov/main/deschutes/home

Finding the trailhead: From Sisters head 10 miles north west on US 20 to Camp Sherman Road (FR 14). Turn right (north) and travel 2.7 miles to the junction with FR 1419. Turn left and go 2.3 miles to another road junction and stop sign. Continue straight (you're now on FR 1420) for another 3.4 miles to the junction with FR 400. Turn right onto FR 400 toward Lower Canyon Creek Campground; continue through the campground to the trailhead parking area. GPS: N44 30.078' / W121 38.455'

The Hike

The Metolius River, known for its world-class fly fishing, originates as a natural spring at the base of Black Butte before winding its way north through the Metolius Basin and into Lake Billy Chinook. Numerous springs, fed via porous volcanic rock high in the Central Cascade Mountains, continue to feed the river along its length, keeping the flow rate fairly steady at 1,200 to 1,800 cubic feet per second.

The Northern Paiute and Tenino Indians were the first known people to inhabit the Metolius Basin. They fished for salmon, hunted deer and small game, and gathered nuts and berries on the slopes of Black Butte. In the mid-nineteenth century several well-known explorers traveled through the area. Among them were Captain

The Metolius River is fed by many natural springs.

John Charles Fremont, who passed through in 1843, and Lieutenant Henry Larcom Abbott, who arrived in 1855 as a surveyor for the Pacific Railroad.

Homesteading in the Metolius Valley didn't occur until 1881. Settlers were attracted to the area by the thick timber and abundant grass that provided good grazing for livestock. The numerous springs and creeks in the valley ensured a

Hikers enjoying Metolius River views.

plentiful supply of water. In 1893, with the passage of the Forest Reserve Act by President Grover Cleveland, the Metolius Valley became part of the Cascade Range Forest Reserve. In 1908 the area was incorporated into Deschutes National Forest.

If you want to explore this beautiful river, the West Metolius River Trail is the easiest way to do it. The trail starts at Lower Canyon Creek Campground, located approximately 20 miles northwest of Sisters, and continues on a scenic journey to Wizard Falls Fish Hatchery. Along the way there is lush streamside greenery,

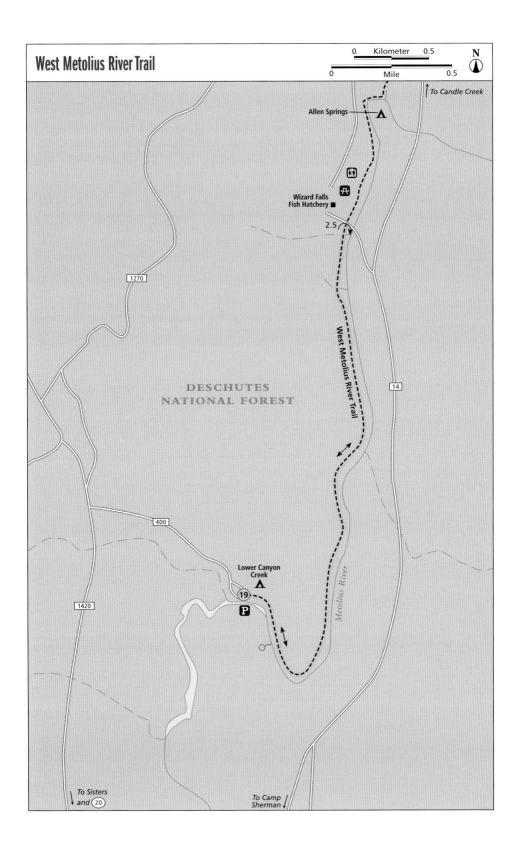

West Metolius River Trail

0 Kilometer 0.5

0 Mile 0.5

N

To Candle Creek

Allen Springs

Wizard Falls
Fish Hatchery

2.5

West Metolius River Trail

14

DESCHUTES
NATIONAL FOREST

1270

400

Metolius River

Lower Canyon
Creek

19

P

1420

To Sisters
and 20

To Camp
Sherman

including pinkish-lavender streambank globemallow and bright orange, fragrant honeysuckle, as well as open forest dotted with purple lupine, crimson columbine, lavender-tufted thistle, and white-headed yarrow. Large ponderosa pines shade the path, and the river's deep rock pools and logs provide a haven for trout and salmon. After 2.5 miles the trail arrives at Wizard Falls Fish Hatchery, which raises almost 3.5 million salmon and trout every year. This is a great place to rest before the return trip to the trailhead. Restrooms and water are available here.

Miles and Directions

0.0 Start this stunning river hike at the wooden trail sign that reads "West Metolius River," located in the Lower Canyon Creek Campground. Another sign indicates that you'll reach Wizard Falls Fish Hatchery in 2.5 miles.

0.3 Look off to the right to view an amazing natural spring that splashes into the river from underground.

2.5 Arrive at Wizard Falls Fish Hatchery. (If you are feeling curious, take the time to explore the fish hatchery before you head back to the trailhead. Water and restrooms are available here.)

5.0 Arrive back at the trailhead.

Option

If you want to enjoy a longer river route, continue on the trail on either the west or east side of the river for about 5 more miles.

Hike Information

Local Information: Sisters Area Chamber of Commerce, 291 E. Main Ave., Sisters; (541) 549-0251; sisterscountry.com

Local Events and Attractions: Sisters Rodeo and Parade, second weekend in June, Sisters; (541) 549-0121; sistersrodeo.com

Sisters Folk Festival, late Sept, Sisters; (541) 549-4979; sistersfolkfestival.org

Restaurants: Sisters Coffee Company, 273 W. Hood Ave., Sisters; (541) 549-0527; sisterscoffee.com

Sisters Bakery, 251 E. Cascade, Sisters; (541) 549-0361; sistersbakery.com

Three Creeks Brewing, 721 S. Desperado Ct., Sisters; (541) 549-1963; three creeksbrewing.com

GREEN TIP

When hiking with your dog, stay in the center of the path and keep Fido close by. Dogs that run loose can harm fragile soils and spread pesky plants by carrying their seeds.

20 Head of the Metolius River

This popular route takes you to a spectacular viewpoint of the natural springs that are the source for the Metolius River.

Start: Metolius Springs trailhead off FR 140
Distance: 0.5-mile out-and-back
Hiking time: About 30 minutes
Difficulty: Easy due to flat paved path
Trail surface: Paved path
Best season: Year-round; snow may be present during the winter months
Other trail users: None
Canine compatibility: Leashed dogs permitted

Land status: Deschutes National Forest
Nearest town: Sisters
Fees and permits: None
Schedule: Open all hours
Maps: USGS Black Butte
Trail contact: Deschutes National Forest, Sisters Ranger District, 201 N. Pine St. and Hwy. 20, Sisters; (541) 549-7700; www.fs.usda.gov/main/deschutes/home

Finding the trailhead: From Sisters travel 10 miles on US 20 to the junction with FR 14. Turn right onto FR 14 toward Camp Sherman. Continue 2.8 miles to a Y junction. Turn right toward the signed campgrounds. Continue 1.6 miles and turn left onto FR 140. Continue 0.1 mile to a paved parking area and the trailhead. GPS: N44 26.037' / W121 38.065'

The Hike

This short trail follows a wide paved path to the bubbling springs that are the source of the Metolius River. The water from these springs flows at a rate of about 50,000 gallons per minute. This clear, spring-fed river flows north from here and then eastward. It eventually joins Lake Billy Chinook, which is also fed by the Deschutes River and the Crooked River. Picnic tables and restrooms are located at the trailhead.

This easy route is framed with a decorative split-rail fence and travels through a parklike stand of ponderosa pine trees to a viewpoint of the Metolius Springs. From the viewpoint you'll have a stunning view of a grassy meadow with snowcapped Mount Jefferson in the background. You'll retrace the same route back to the trailhead.

Miles and Directions

0.0 Start hiking on the wheelchair-accessible paved path.
0.25 Arrive at a viewpoint of the headwaters of the Metolius River. Turn around and retrace the same route back to the trailhead.
0.5 Arrive back at the trailhead.

Scenic views include the Metolius River with Mount Jefferson in the background.

Hike Information

Local Information: Sisters Area Chamber of Commerce, 291 E. Main Ave., Sisters; (866) 549-0251; sisterscountry.com

Local Events and Attractions: Sisters Rodeo and Parade, second weekend in June, Sisters; (541) 549-0121; sistersrodeo.com

Sisters Folk Festival, late Sept, Sisters; (541) 549-4979; sistersfolkfestival.org

Restaurants: Sisters Coffee Company, 273 W. Hood Ave., Sisters; (541) 549-0527; sisterscoffee.com

Sisters Bakery, 251 E. Cascade, Sisters; (541) 549-0361; sistersbakery.com

Three Creeks Brewing, 721 S. Desperado Ct., Sisters; (541) 549-1963; three creeksbrewing.com

GREEN TIP
Stay on the trail. Cutting through from one part of
a switchback to another can destroy fragile plant life.

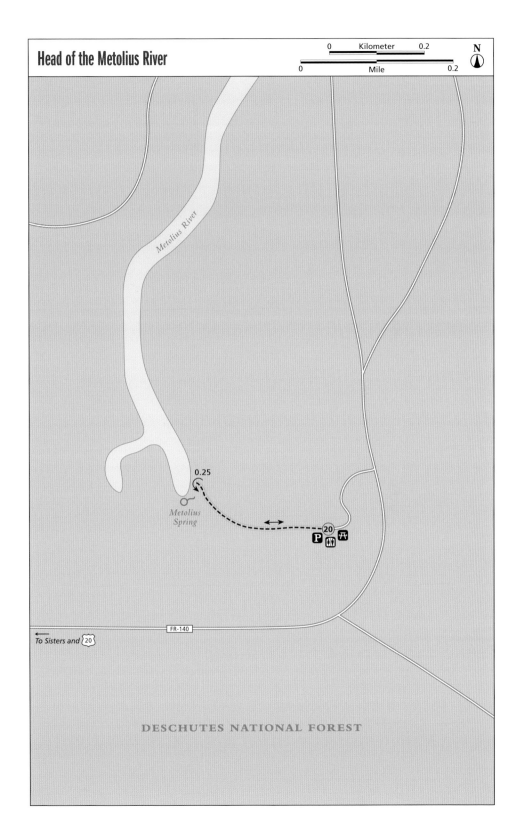

Head of the Metolius River

0   Kilometer   0.2

0   Mile   0.2

N

Metolius River

0.25

Metolius
Spring

20

P

A

FR-140

To Sisters and 20

DESCHUTES NATIONAL FOREST

21 Black Butte

This trail leads to the top of one of Central Oregon's best-known landmarks, 6,436-foot Black Butte. The summit includes three historic fire lookouts and fantastic views of several Cascade peaks to the west. Interpretive signs en route to the summit point out native plant and tree species.

Start: Black Butte trailhead off FR 700
Distance: 3.8-mile out-and-back
Hiking time: 3 to 5 hours
Difficulty: Difficult due to the steep ascent to the summit of Black Butte
Trail surface: Dirt path
Best season: Year-round; snow may be present during the winter months
Other trail users: None
Canine compatibility: Leashed dogs permitted
Land status: Deschutes National Forest
Nearest town: Sisters

Fees and permits: A Northwest Forest Pass is required for a small fee. You can purchase a pass at www.fs.usda.gov/main/deschutes/passes-permits/recreation, or by calling (800) 270-7504.
Schedule: Open all hours
Maps: USGS Black Butte
Trail contact: Deschutes National Forest, Sisters Ranger District, 201 N. Pine St. and Hwy. 20, Sisters; (541) 549-7700; www.fs.usda.gov/main/deschutes/home

Finding the trailhead: Travel 6 miles northwest of Sisters on US 20 and turn right onto Green Ridge Road (FR 11). Go 3.8 miles to FR 1110. Turn left onto FR 1110 and travel 4.2 miles to the junction with FR 700. Turn right and continue 1.1 miles to a large parking area and the trailhead. GPS: N44 23.679' / W121 38.839'

The Hike

Black Butte rises 6,436 feet above the Central Oregon landscape. This well-known geological landmark, a 1.5-million-year-old stratovolcano, was created by numerous basaltic lava flows over hundreds of years. Because Black Butte stands in the rain shadow of the Cascade Mountains, it has not been exposed to the eroding forces of wind and water like its neighboring peaks and has therefore managed to maintain its conical shape.

Black Butte is located approximately 10 miles northwest of Sisters, a typically Western town established in 1888. Some of the first explorers to pass through the Sisters area mentioned Black Butte in their journals. That old trail has most likely faded away, but today there is a relatively new path to Black Butte's summit. The 1.9-mile trail begins at the end of FR 700 and winds through a dry, open forest of ponderosa and whitebark pine and Douglas, subalpine, and grand fir. Signposts along the trail point out these tree species as well as other indigenous plants including squaw currant, bitterbrush, and pinemat manzanita. Small groves of quaking aspens

This historic cupola fire tower was built in 1934 and took more than 1,000 packhorse loads of material to build.

have also staked out territory along the trail. These silvery, shimmering trees have one of the largest footholds in the West and can be found from the Atlantic to the Pacific Coast.

After about a mile the trail becomes steeper, and soon there are gorgeous, sweeping views of Mount Washington and other Cascade peaks rising majestically to the west. At the butte's summit there are signs indicating the names and elevations of the prominent peaks. There are also historic fire towers you can view. Soak up the sun and the views before you turn around and head back to your vehicle.

Nice view of Mount Washington from the summit of Black Butte.

Miles and Directions

0.0   Start hiking on the signed trail.

0.4   There's a great view of Mount Washington to the left.

1.8   Pass the old cupola and lookout tower on your right. This historic tower, built in 1934, took more than 1,000 packhorse-loads of material to build.

1.9   Arrive at the 6,436-foot summit of Black Butte and the turnaround point. Before you leave, enjoy views of Broken Top (9,175 feet), South Sister (10,358 feet), North Sister (10,085 feet), Belknap Crater (6,872 feet), and Mount Washington (7,794 feet) to the southwest; and to the northwest, views of Haystack Butte (5,523 feet), Three Fingered

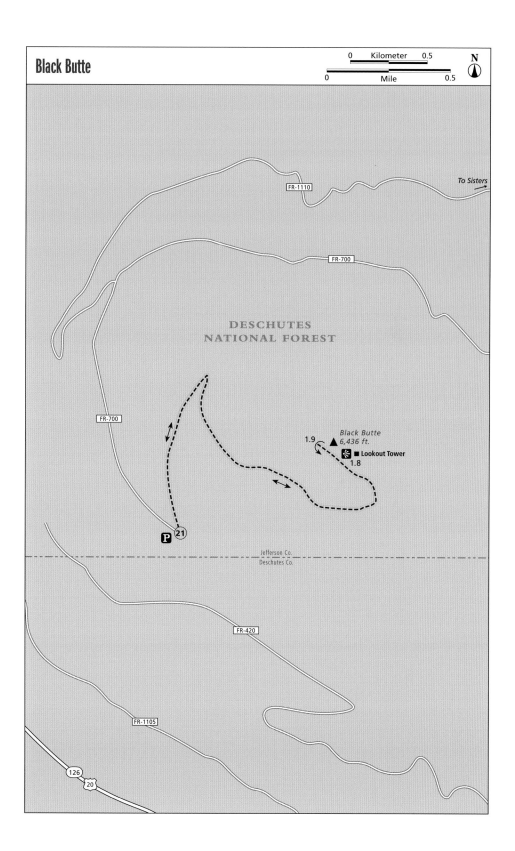

Black Butte

0   Kilometer   0.5

0   Mile   0.5

N

FR-1110

To Sisters

FR-700

DESCHUTES
NATIONAL FOREST

FR-700

Black Butte
▲ 6,436 ft.
1.9
■ Lookout Tower
1.8

P 21

Jefferson Co.
Deschutes Co.

FR-420

FR-1105

126
20

One of the historic fire towers on the summit of Black Butte.

Jack (7,841 feet), Mount Jefferson (10,497 feet), Mount Hood (11,235 feet), and Mount Adams (12,326 feet). Retrace the same route back to the trailhead.

3.8 Arrive back at the trailhead.

Hike Information

Local Information: Sisters Area Chamber of Commerce, 291 E. Main Ave., Sisters; (541) 549-0251; sisterscountry.com

Local Events and Attractions: Sisters Rodeo and Parade, second weekend in June, Sisters; (541) 549-0121; sistersrodeo.com

Sisters Folk Festival, late Sept, Sisters; (541) 549-4979; sistersfolkfestival.org

Restaurants: Sisters Coffee Company, 273 W. Hood Ave., Sisters; (541) 549-0527; sisterscoffee.com

Sisters Bakery, 251 E. Cascade, Sisters; (541) 549-0361; sistersbakery.com

Three Creeks Brewing, 721 S. Desperado Ct., Sisters; (541) 549-1963; three creeksbrewing.com

22 Black Crater

This trail winds its way through a mountain-hemlock forest to the craggy red-cinder summit of Black Crater. At the prominent summit you can enjoy sweeping views of the snow-topped Three Sisters Mountains, Mount Washington, and the surrounding lava flows and craters that are reminders of this area's violent volcanic past.

Start: Black Crater trailhead off McKenzie Highway (OR 242)
Distance: 7.2-mile out-and-back
Hiking time: 3 to 4 hours
Difficulty: Difficult due to the very strenuous climb to the summit of Black Crater
Trail surface: Dirt path and lava scree
Best season: July through Oct
Other trail users: None
Canine compatibility: Leashed dogs permitted
Land status: Three Sisters Wilderness

Nearest town: Sisters
Fees and permits: A free self-issue wilderness permit is required and is available at the trailhead.
Schedule: Open all hours
Maps: USGS Black Crater and Mount Washington
Trail contact: Deschutes National Forest, Sisters Ranger District, 201 N. Pine St. and Hwy. 20, Sisters; (541) 549-7700; www.fs.usda.gov/main/deschutes/home

Finding the trailhead: From Sisters travel west on the McKenzie Highway (OR 242) for 0.2 mile to a stop sign. Turn right and continue 11.5 miles on OR 242 to the Black Crater trailhead, on the left (south) side of the road. The turnoff Is easy to miss because It Is only signed with a very small hiker sign. *Note:* Depending on winter snow conditions, the McKenzie Highway may not open until July. GPS: N44 17.085' / W121 45.947'

The Hike

Central Oregon is truly the land of volcanoes, and the Sisters vicinity is perhaps its most shining example. One incredible hike is along the Black Crater Trail, which leads to the summit of 7,251-foot Black Crater. The difficult path, which climbs to the craggy, double-pinnacled summit, is a test of both strength and endurance.

The trail begins as a series of switchbacks through an old burn area that is the charred remains of the devastating Mill Fire that burned 24,000 acres in the summer of 2017. The fire was started by a lightning strike and many Sisters residents had to be evacuated.

As you hike up this trail, you'll catch glimpses of Mount Washington in the distance. After 2.6 miles you'll leave the burn area and enter a predominantly mountain hemlock forest. Mountain hemlock can be found growing at elevations of 3,500 to 6,000 feet and is often confused with western hemlock. The hardy

Ken Skeen and Tiz hiking to the summit of Black Crater.

tree is differentiated from the western hemlock by its thick needles that fan out in bushy clusters. It also has 2-inch-long cones and blue-green foliage. In contrast, the western hemlock has flat needles that are shaped in an open spray, cones that are an inch or less in length, and yellow-green foliage. Mountain hemlocks are also characterized by their deep, furrowed bark and are usually the first trees to grow at timberline. It's not uncommon for a mature branch to touch the ground and take root as a new tree. The parent tree then shelters the new tree from the harsh high-altitude environment. As you climb higher notice the crooked whitebark pine trees (shaped by the prevailing southeasterly winds). Inhabiting elevations above 5,500 feet, these tough trees are sprinkled across hundreds of miles of high-country land-scape from central British Columbia to California and as far east as Wyoming. At the edge of the treeline, these trees grow 40 to 80 feet tall and have thick, stout trunks with widespread branches. Above timberline, whitebark pines take on a totally dif-ferent appearance. Growing to heights of only 5 to 12 feet, the trees become more

Tiz on the summit of Black Crater.

shrub-like. The branches and trunk are often twisted and bent and are known as krummholz—German for "crooked wood." At higher elevations the trees become even smaller and are often referred to as alpine scrub.

As the trail nears the summit, it crosses an alpine-like meadow sprinkled with purple, yellow, and white bouquets of wildflowers. At the summit are two prominent pinnacles that rise above the crater. From these spires you can enjoy a panoramic view of the Three Sisters to the south and Belknap Crater and Mounts Washington, Jefferson, and Hood to the north. The spectacular scenery makes it obvious why so many other hikers are attracted to this spot. If you're looking for solitude, hike the trail on a weekday.

Miles and Directions

0.0   Start hiking on Black Crater Trail 58. (*Note:* Be sure to fill out a free wilderness permit at the trailhead sign.)

3.6   Reach the summit and your turnaround point. Retrace the same route back to your starting point.

7.2   Arrive back at the trailhead.

The view from the summit takes in the Black Crater Trail as well as numerous lofty peaks in the distance.

Hike Information

Local Information: Sisters Area Chamber of Commerce, 291 E. Main Ave., Sisters; (541) 549-0251; sisterscountry.com

Local Events and Attractions: Sisters Rodeo and Parade, second weekend in June, Sisters; (541) 549-0121; sistersrodeo.com

Sisters Folk Festival, late Sept, Sisters; (541) 549-4979; sistersfolkfestival.org

Restaurants: Sisters Coffee Company, 273 W. Hood Ave., Sisters; (541) 549-0527; sisterscoffee.com

Sisters Bakery, 251 E. Cascade, Sisters; (541) 549-0361; sistersbakery.com

Three Creeks Brewing, 721 S. Desperado Ct., Sisters; (541) 549-1963; three creeksbrewing.com

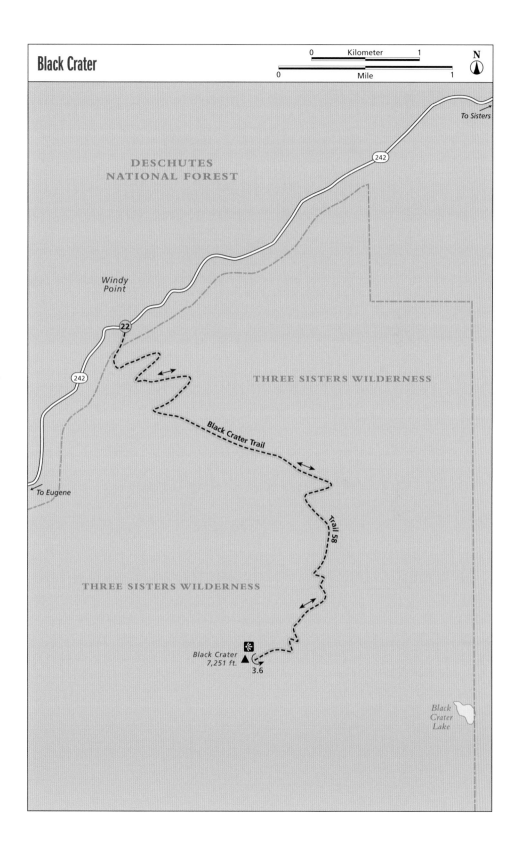

Black Crater

0 Kilometer 1

0 Mile 1

N

To Sisters

DESCHUTES
NATIONAL FOREST

242

Windy
Point

22

242

THREE SISTERS WILDERNESS

Black Crater Trail

To Eugene

Trail 58

THREE SISTERS WILDERNESS

Black Crater
7,251 ft.

3.6

Black
Crater
Lake

23 Lava River Trail–Dee Wright Observatory

This hike takes you on a tour of the moonlike landscape of the Yapoah Crater Lava Flow in the Mount Washington Wilderness.

Start: Lava River trailhead off McKenzie Highway (OR 242)
Distance: 0.5-mile lollipop loop
Hiking time: 30 minutes to 1 hour
Difficulty: Easy due to paved path and flat terrain
Trail surface: Paved path and stairs that lead to Dee Wright Observatory
Best season: July through Oct
Other trail users: None

Canine compatibility: Leashed dogs permitted
Land status: Deschutes National Forest
Nearest town: Sisters
Fees and permits: None
Schedule: Open all hours
Maps: USGS Mount Washington or Black Butte
Trail contact: Deschutes National Forest, Sisters Ranger District, 201 N. Pine St. and Hwy. 20, Sisters; (541) 549-7700; www.fs.usda.gov/main/deschutes/home

Finding the trailhead: From Sisters turn west onto the McKenzie Highway (OR 242) and travel 14.5 miles to a gravel pullout on the left side of the road, marked by a brown hiker symbol. **Note:** Depending on the winter snow conditions, the McKenzie Highway may not open until July. GPS: N44 15.613' / W121 48.094'

The Hike

This hike explores the western edge of the Yapoah Crater Lava Flow. This incredible lava flow, 8 miles long and a mile wide, is thought to have erupted from Yapoah Crater as recently as 2,700 years ago. The lava that makes up this flow is called AA lava (pronounced ah-ah) or black lava. This type of lava is made up of basalt and has a rough, jagged surface. This rough surface is caused when the upper layers of lava cool quickly while the lower layers are still flowing. You'll follow a paved path through the lava flow on a short 0.5-mile lollipop loop. When you finish the hike, you can explore the Dee Wright Observatory. The observatory was built by the Civilian Conservation Corps (CCC) and named for an early-1900s Forest Service packer and mountain guide. The observatory's arched windows frame eleven Cascade peaks.

Miles and Directions

0.0   Start the hike by crossing the highway (use caution) and turning right onto the paved Lava River Trail. (**Option:** You have the option to walk up a series of short switchbacks to tour the Dee Wright Observatory.)

View of Mount Washington from the top of the Dee Wright Observatory.

0.1 Turn left to begin the loop portion of the trail.
0.2 The trail forks. Stay to the left.
0.4 Finish the loop. Go left to return to the trailhead.
0.5 Arrive back at the trailhead. Continue straight and walk up the paved spiral path to view the Dee Wright Observatory. After enjoying the views, head back to the parking area.

The Dee Wright Observatory was built in 1935 by the Civilian Conservation Corps (CCC).

Hike Information

Local Information: Sisters Area Chamber of Commerce, 291 E. Main Ave., Sisters; (541) 549-0251; sisterscountry.com

Local Events and Attractions: Sisters Rodeo and Parade, second weekend in June, Sisters; (541) 549-0121; sistersrodeo.com

Sisters Folk Festival, late Sept, Sisters; (541) 549-4979; sistersfolkfestival.org

Restaurants: Sisters Coffee Company, 273 W. Hood Ave., Sisters; (541) 549-0527; sisterscoffee.com

Sisters Bakery, 251 E. Cascade, Sisters; (541) 549-0361; sistersbakery.com

Three Creeks Brewing, 721 S. Desperado Ct., Sisters; (541) 549-1963; threecreeksbrewing.com

Lava River Trail—Dee Wright Observatory

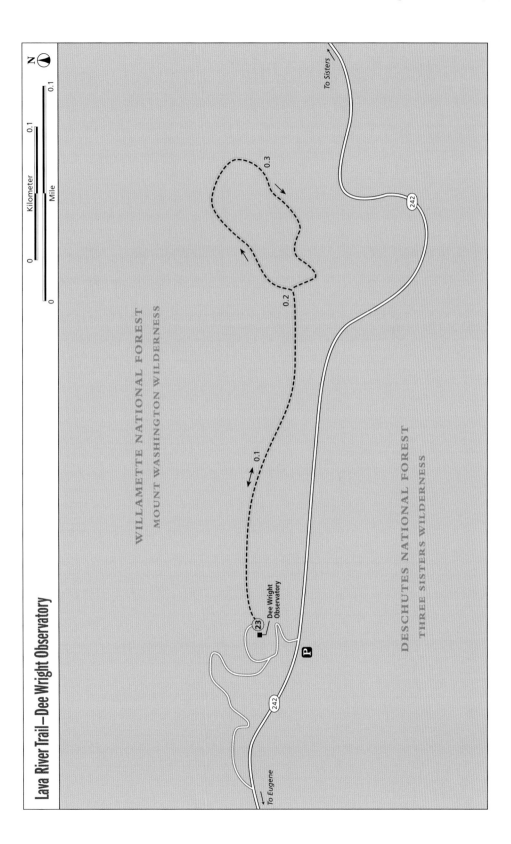

N

Kilometer
0   0.1

Mile
0   0.1

WILLAMETTE NATIONAL FOREST
MOUNT WASHINGTON WILDERNESS

DESCHUTES NATIONAL FOREST
THREE SISTERS WILDERNESS

To Sisters

242

0.3

0.2

0.1

23
Dee Wright
Observatory

P

242

To Eugene

24 Little Belknap Crater

On this route you will follow the Pacific Crest Trail as it passes through a moonlike landscape on its way to the summit of Little Belknap Crater. From the summit you can enjoy views of the Three Sisters, Mount Washington, Black Crater, and many other Cascade peaks.

Start: Pacific Crest Trail 2000 trailhead off McKenzie Highway (OR 242)
Distance: 5.0-mile out-and-back
Hiking time: 3 to 4 hours
Difficulty: Difficult due to rough trail surface and significant elevation gain
Trail surface: Dirt path and lava scree
Best season: July through Oct
Other trail users: None
Canine compatibility: Leashed dogs permitted. However, this hike is not dog friendly because of the very sharp lava scree that can cut your dog's feet and the very hot conditions in the summer months with no shade or water.
Land status: Mount Washington Wilderness
Nearest town: Sisters
Fees and permits: A free self-issue wilderness permit is required and is available at the trailhead.
Schedule: Open all hours
Maps: USGS Mount Washington
Trail contact: Deschutes National Forest, Sisters Ranger District, 201 N. Pine St. and Hwy 20, Sisters; (541) 549-7700; www.fs.usda.gov/main/deschutes/home

Finding the trailhead: From Sisters turn west onto McKenzie Highway (OR 242). Go 0.2 mile to a stop sign. Turn right and travel 15.1 miles west to the Pacific Crest Trail 2000 trailhead, located on the right (north) side of the road. (A very small "hiker" sign marks the trailhead.) *Note:* Depending on winter snow conditions, the McKenzie Highway may not open until July. GPS: N44 15.589' / W121 48.305'

The Hike

The rugged character of Central Oregon's lava country is nowhere better represented than on this hike to the summit of Little Belknap Crater. The rich history of the area begins with the highway to the trailhead. The McKenzie Highway (OR 242) is a gorgeous scenic byway with spectacular views of mountains, lava fields, and endless blue sky—a great introduction to the hike you're about to take.

When gold was discovered in eastern Oregon and Idaho in the 1860s, settlers made a push to find a route that connected the Willamette Valley on the west side of the Cascades to the land on the east. In 1862 Felix Scott and his brother Marion led a party of forty men, sixty oxen, and 900 head of cattle and horses across McKenzie Pass, blazing what would later become the Scott Trail. An extremely rough trail, the Scott Trail required almost 5 days to travel from Eugene in the Willamette Valley to the small town of Sisters in Central Oregon. For future travelers, a toll road was

Ken Skeen at the summit of Little Belknap Crater with Mount Washington in the background.

built in 1872 that traveled up Lost Creek Canyon, traversed the rough lava beds, and ended at the Deschutes River.

Today the road is paved and toll-free. It also happens to pass the Dee Wright Observatory (14.5 miles west of Sisters), built by the Civilian Conservation Corps and named for an early 1900s Forest Service packer and mountain guide. The observatory's arched windows frame eleven Cascade peaks. A paved half-mile walkway offers an easy means to explore the eerie moonscape of the Yapoah Crater Lava Flow. The trail is complemented by interpretive signs detailing the area's unique geology. Signs of the old McKenzie Highway, which once crossed the flow, are visible from this vantage point.

When you've had enough of the observatory, continue on to the trailhead for Little Belknap Crater. The trail (95 percent of which is the Pacific Crest Trail), leads through the heart of the Mount Washington Wilderness and its rugged lava formations, craters, and extinct volcanoes. The route begins rather innocently as it

Ken Skeen hiking to the summit of Little Belknap Crater.

winds through an open forest. But within a mile, things change drastically. Soon the forest is replaced by a grayish-black lava flow practically devoid of life, except for the rare hardy tree that has managed to sink its roots through the jumbled basalt rocks.

The flow was created more than 2,900 years ago when hot liquid basalt poured from Belknap Crater, the large cinder cone to the west. Approximately 20 years later a second eruption sprang out of Little Belknap Crater, located directly north of the trailhead. A third phase of eruptions occurred a little more than a thousand years later from the northeast base of Belknap Crater, releasing lava 9 miles west into the McKenzie River Valley.

After 2.2 miles of hiking through this mysterious maze of rock, you come to a trail junction and go right. In 0.2 mile you pass a deep lava tube on your left. If you approach the edge of the tube and look in (be careful—it's quite a drop-off), you can feel the cool air escaping from deep within the earth.

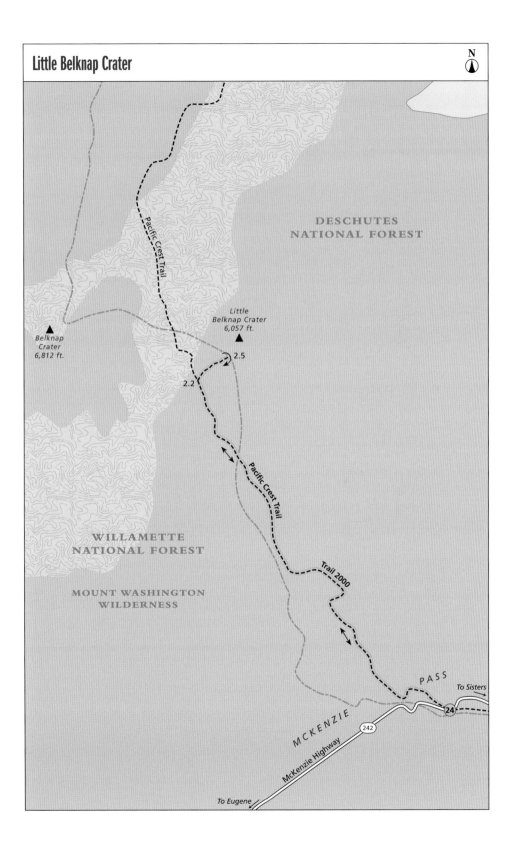

N

DESCHUTES
NATIONAL FOREST

Pacific Crest Trail

Little
Belknap Crater
6,057 ft.

Belknap
Crater
6,812 ft.

2.5

2.2

Pacific Crest Trail

Trail 2000

WILLAMETTE
NATIONAL FOREST

MOUNT WASHINGTON
WILDERNESS

PASS

To Sisters

24

MCKENZIE

242

McKenzie Highway

To Eugene

From the lava tube, hike a steep and dramatic 0.1 mile to the top of Little Belknap Crater. The trail surface is loose and crumbly, and piles of gray rock mingle with the bright-red cinders that form much of the crater. When you reach the top, you can enjoy magnificent views of Belknap Crater, Mount Washington, Black Crater, and the Three Sisters Mountains. The summit of Little Belknap Crater is your turnaround point. If you're backpacking, continue on the Pacific Crest Trail as it winds its way north through the magnificent lava country of the Mount Washington Wilderness.

Miles and Directions

0.0 Start hiking on the signed Pacific Crest Trail 2000. (**Note:** Be sure to fill out the free self-issue wilderness permit at the trailhead.)

0.8 Begin walking on the lava flow.

2.2 Come to a trail junction and turn right to hike to the summit of Little Belknap Crater.

2.4 Pass a lava tube on your left.

2.5 Reach the summit and enjoy sweeping views of Belknap Crater, Mount Washington, Black Crater, and the Three Sisters. Turn around here and retrace your route back to the trailhead. **Option:** Continue north on the Pacific Crest Trail and explore more of the Mount Washington Wilderness. Return to your starting point on the same route.

5.0 Arrive back at the trailhead.

Option

After summiting Little Belknap Crater, return to the junction with the Pacific Crest Trail and turn right. Continue north on the Pacific Crest Trail and explore more of the Mount Washington Wilderness.

Hike Information

Local Information: Sisters Area Chamber of Commerce, 291 E. Main Ave., Sisters; (541) 549-0251 ; sisterscountry.com

Local Events and Attractions: Sisters Rodeo and Parade, second weekend in June, Sisters; (541) 549-0121; sistersrodeo.com

Sisters Folk Festival, late Sept, Sisters; (541) 549-4979; sistersfolkfestival.org

Restaurants: Sisters Coffee Company, 273 W. Hood Ave., Sisters; (541) 549-0527; sisterscoffee.com

Sisters Bakery, 251 E. Cascade, Sisters; (541) 549-0361; sistersbakery.com

Three Creeks Brewing, 721 S. Desperado Ct., Sisters; (541) 549-1963; three creeksbrewing.com

25 Hand Lake

This short hike takes you through a scented pine forest to a small alpine lake with gorgeous views of snowcapped Mount Washington.

Start: Hand Lake trailhead off McKenzie Highway (OR 242)
Distance: 1.0-mile out-and-back
Hiking time: About 1 hour
Difficulty: Easy due to well-graded path and fairly flat terrain
Trail surface: Dirt path
Best season: July through Oct
Other trail users: None
Canine compatibility: Leashed dogs permitted
Land status: Deschutes National Forest

Nearest town: Sisters
Fees and permits: A free self-issue wilderness permit is required and is available at the trailhead.
Schedule: Open all hours
Maps: USGS North Sister
Trail contact: Deschutes National Forest, Sisters Ranger District, 201 N. Pine St. and Hwy. 20, Sisters; (541) 549-7700; www.fs.usda.gov/main/deschutes/home

Finding the trailhead: From Sisters turn west onto the McKenzie Highway (OR 242) and travel 19.4 miles to a gravel pullout on the left side of the road, marked by a brown hiker symbol. GPS: N44 13.449' / W121 52.308'

The Hike

Begin this hike by crossing the highway (use caution) to the signed trailhead, where you can obtain a free self-issue wilderness permit. Start hiking on a dirt path as it descends through a thick stand of lodgepole pine dotted with purple lupine. After 0.5 mile you'll emerge from the woods into a scenic high alpine meadow. Take time to explore the rustic three-sided wood shelter and to walk on a side trail down to the lake's edge. From here you'll have outstanding views of the pointy summit of Mount Washington. Retrace the same route back to the trailhead. Be armed with mosquito repellent on this hike.

Miles and Directions

0.0 Cross OR 242 and start walking on the dirt path.
0.5 Arrive at a three-sided wood shelter. Follow a side trail down to the lake's edge. Retrace the same route back to the trailhead.
1.0 Arrive back at the trailhead.

Hike Information

Local Information: Sisters Area Chamber of Commerce, 291 E. Main Ave., Sisters; (541) 549-0251 ; sisterscountry.com

Mount Washington peeks over the trees behind Hand Lake.

Local Events and Attractions: Sisters Rodeo and Parade, second weekend in June, Sisters; (541) 549-0121; sistersrodeo.com

Sisters Folk Festival, late Sept, Sisters; (541) 549-4979; sistersfolkfestival.org

Restaurants: Sisters Coffee Company, 273 W. Hood Ave., Sisters; (541) 549-0527; sisterscoffee.com

Sisters Bakery, 251 E. Cascade, Sisters; (541) 549-0361; sistersbakery.com

Three Creeks Brewing, 721 S. Desperado Ct., Sisters; (541) 549-1963; three creeksbrewing.com

GREEN TIP
Carry a reusable water container that you fill at the tap. Bottled water is expensive; lots of petroleum is used to make the plastic bottles, and they're a disposal nightmare.

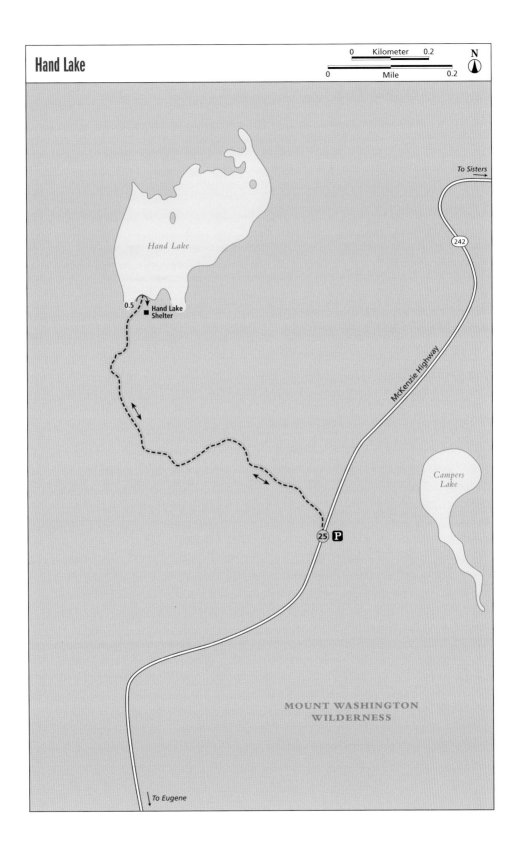

Hand Lake

0   Kilometer   0.2

0   Mile   0.2

N

To Sisters

242

McKenzie Highway

Hand Lake

0.5

Hand Lake
Shelter

Campers
Lake

25 P

MOUNT WASHINGTON
WILDERNESS

To Eugene

26 Canyon Creek Meadows

This popular loop route takes you past Jack Lake and on a tour of a high alpine meadow with bubbling Canyon Creek flowing through it. In addition, you'll enjoy spectacular views of the jagged spires of Three Fingered Jack.

Start: Canyon Creek Meadows trailhead at Jack Lake
Distance: 5.2-mile loop
Hiking time: 2.5 to 3.5 hours
Difficulty: Easy due to smooth trail surface
Trail surface: Dirt path
Best season: Late June through Oct
Other trail users: None
Canine compatibility: Leashed dogs permitted
Land status: Mount Jefferson Wilderness
Nearest town: Sisters

Fees and permits: A Northwest Forest Pass is required for a small fee. You can purchase a pass online at www.fs.usda.gov/main/r6/passes-permits or by calling (800) 270-7504.
Schedule: Open all hours
Maps: USGS Three Fingered Jack and Marion Lake
Trail contact: Deschutes National Forest, Sisters Ranger District, 201 N. Pine St. and Hwy. 20, Sisters; (541) 549-7700; www.fs.usda.gov/main/deschutes/home

Finding the trailhead: From Sisters travel west on US 20 for 12 miles to Jack Lake Road (FR 12). Turn right and travel 4.3 miles on Jack Lake Road to the junction with FR 1230. Turn left on FR 1230 and go 1.7 miles. At the next road junction, bear left on FR 1234 and continue 5 miles to the trailhead. GPS: N44 23.679' / W121 38.839'

The Hike

High mountain scenery is the highlight of this popular trail. The route takes you past Jack Lake and then enters spectacular Canyon Creek Meadows. Jack Lake covers about 7 acres and is host to a nice campground.

This hike offers you opportunities to view meadows filled with a profusion of bright purple lupine and brilliant red Indian paintbrush blooms in the summer. Along this trail you will also have the opportunity to enjoy a stunning view of the craggy spires of 7,841-foot Three Fingered Jack—named in honor of Joaquin Murietta, an aspiring gold rusher with a mutilated, three-fingered hand. The spires rise abruptly out of Central Oregon's Mount Jefferson Wilderness to form a geologic slide of time. Hundreds of thousands of years ago, the mountain—formed by hot basaltic lava flows—resembled a broad, dome-shaped cone. Since that time, volcanic activity and glaciations have left the southern side of the peak a skeleton of its previous majesty. Today the formation is what geologists call a shield volcano. Bring plenty of mosquito repellent with you on this hike. Also, try to hike this trail during the week to avoid the weekend crowds.

Scenic Canyon Creek.

Miles and Directions

0.0   Start hiking on the singletrack trail signed for Canyon Creek Meadows. The trail travels past Jack Lake.

0.4   Turn toward Canyon Creek on Trail 4010. This trail is marked as a one-way loop.

2.2   Arrive at a trail junction at Canyon Creek and a large, picturesque meadow. Turn right and continue on the one-way trail.

Late summer wildflowers.

2.5 Cross a bridge.
2.9 Cross the creek.
3.4 At the trail junction, turn right onto Trail #4014.
4.8 Turn left onto Trail #4010 toward Jack Lake.
5.2 Arrive back at the trailhead.

Canyon Creek Meadows

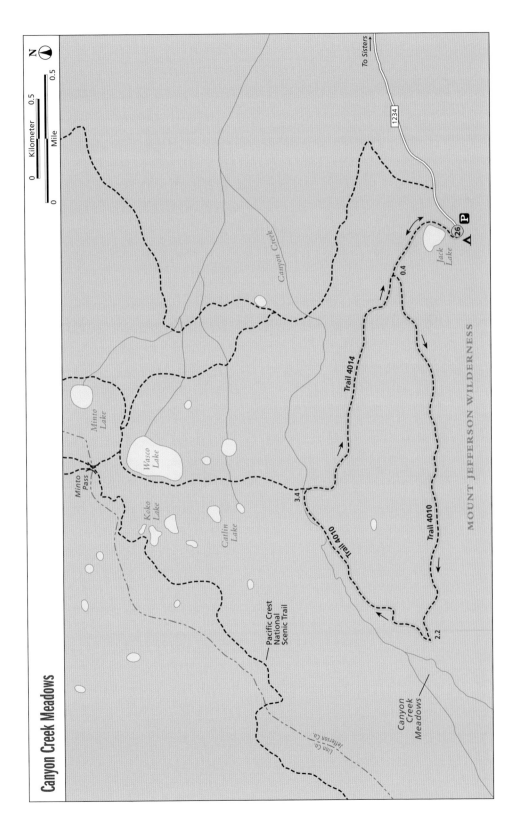

N

Kilometer
0   0.5
0   0.5
Mile

To Sisters

1234

P
26

Jack
Lake

0.4

Trail 4014

3.4

Canyon Creek

Minto
Lake

Minto
Pass

Wasco
Lake

Koko
Lake

Catlin
Lake

Trail 4010

Trail 4010

2.2

Pacific Crest
National
Scenic Trail

Linn Co.
Jefferson Co.

Canyon
Creek
Meadows

MOUNT JEFFERSON WILDERNESS

Ken Skeen with Zane and Tiz admiring Jack Lake.

Hike Information

Local Information: Sisters Area Chamber of Commerce, 291 E. Main Ave., Sisters; (541) 549-0251; sisterscountry.com

Local Events and Attractions: Sisters Rodeo and Parade, second weekend in June, Sisters; (541) 549-0121; sistersrodeo.com

Sisters Folk Festival, late Sept, Sisters; (541) 549-4979; sistersfolkfestival.org

Restaurants: Sisters Coffee Company, 273 W. Hood Ave., Sisters; (541) 549-0527; sisterscoffee.com

Sisters Bakery, 251 E. Cascade, Sisters; (541) 549-0361; sistersbakery.com

Three Creeks Brewing, 721 S. Desperado Ct., Sisters; (541) 549-1963; three creeksbrewing.com

27 Matthieu Lakes Loop

This is a scenic mountain lake hike where you will complete a loop to North and South Matthieu Lakes and then descend an open ridge with nice views of North Sister and other Central Cascade peaks. These high lakes are great for swimming in July and August and have established campsites if you decide you want to turn this popular day hike into an overnight trip.

Start: Lava Camp Lake Trail #4060 trailhead
Distance: 6.2-mile lollipop loop
Hiking time: 3 to 4 hours
Difficulty: Moderate due to 880 feet of elevation gain
Trail surface: Dirt path
Best season: July through Oct
Other trail users: None
Canine compatibility: Dogs permitted. They must be leashed July 15 through Sept 15.
Land status: National forest and wilderness area
Nearest town: Sisters

Fees and permits: A Central Cascades Wilderness Permit is required for day and overnight visitors between June 15 and Oct 15. You can reserve a permit at Recreation.gov or by calling (877) 444-6777. A self-issue wilderness permit is required at the trailhead.
Schedule: Open all hours
Maps: USGS North Sister
Trail contact: Deschutes National Forest, Sisters Ranger District, 201 N. Pine St. and Hwy. 20, Sisters; (541) 549-7700; www.fs.usda.gov/main/deschutes/home

Finding the trailhead: From US 20 in Sisters, turn onto OR 242 (McKenzie Pass Highway) for 14.2 miles. Turn left at the Lava Camp Lake and the Pacific Crest Trail sign. Continue 0.3 mile and turn right into the signed Pacific Crest Trail parking area. GPS: N44 14.116' / W121 33.71'

The Hike

This is a great hike to bring your dogs and to enjoy a cool swim on a hot summer day! The hike starts on the Lava Camp Lake Trail and then intersects with the Pacific Crest Trail after 0.2 mile. If you are hiking in June or July, you may still see snowmelt ponds along this section of the trail. At 0.9 mile you'll Intersect with the North Matthieu Lake Trail. After 1.1 miles the trail skirts a lava field and then starts climbing. After 2.1 miles you'll arrive at a spur trail that takes you to the scenic shores of North Matthieu Lake. If you feel like exploring, follow the perimeter trail around the lake. After enjoying the lake, you'll continue climbing on a series of switchbacks until you intersect with the Pacific Crest Trail. Continue on the Pacific Crest Trail until you intersect with a spur trail leading to South Matthieu Lake. Once you reach the lakeshore, you'll have a nice view of North Sister. From here you'll continue on the Pacific Crest Trail. As you continue on the trail you'll descend a large, open ridge with nice views of the Central Cascade peaks. You'll continue descending on the Pacific Crest Trail until you reach the junction with Lava Camp Lake Trail #4060, which you'll follow back to the trailhead.

Rahul Ravel enjoying the lake scenery.

Miles and Directions

0.0 Start hiking on the signed Lava Camp Lake Trail #4060.

0.2 Turn left (south) on the signed Pacific Crest Trail #2000.

0.9 Turn right onto North Matthieu Lake Trail #4062.

1.1 Start hiking on the edge of a lava field past several snowmelt ponds. Snow can be present on the trail in early July.

2.0 Turn right onto a spur trail that takes you to the shore of North Matthieu Lake.

2.1 Arrive at North Matthieu Lake shore. After viewing the lake, return to the main trail.

3.0 Arrive at an intersection with the Pacific Crest Trail #2000.

3.1 At the trail junction turn right to view South Matthieu Lake. You will also have nice views of North Sister. After viewing the lake, return to the main trail.

5.3 At the trail junction, turn right and continue hiking on the Pacific Crest Trail #2000.

6.0 Turn right at the signed Lava Camp Lake Trail #4060.

6.2 Arrive back at the trailhead.

Hike Information

Local Information: Sisters Area Chamber of Commerce, 291 E. Main Ave., Sisters; (541) 549-0251 ; sisterscountry.com

Local Events and Attractions: Sisters Rodeo and Parade, second weekend in June, Sisters; (541) 549-0121; sistersrodeo.com

Sisters Folk Festival, late Sept, Sisters; (541) 549-4979; sistersfolkfestival.org

Restaurants: Sisters Coffee Company, 273 W. Hood Ave., Sisters; (541) 549-0527; sisterscoffee.com

Sisters Bakery, 251 E. Cascade, Sisters; (541) 549-0361; sistersbakery.com

Three Creeks Brewing, 721 S. Desperado Ct., Sisters; (541) 549-1963; three creeksbrewing.com

Matthieu Lakes Loop

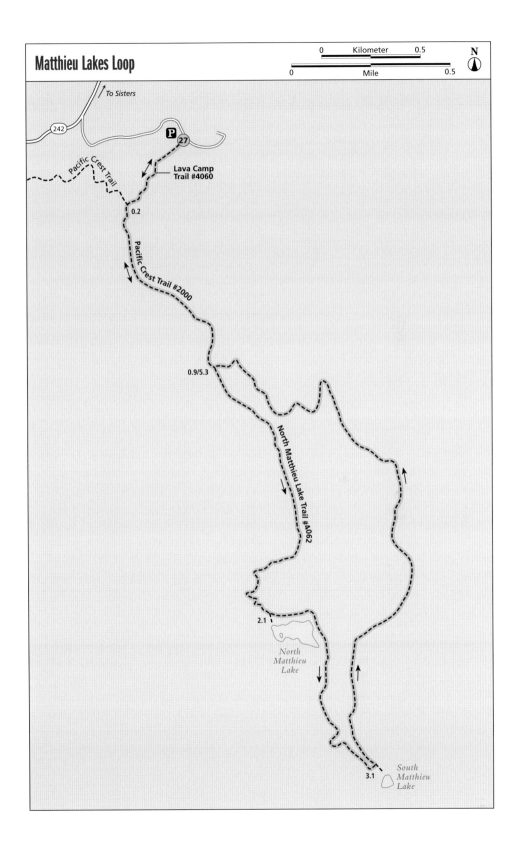

0   Kilometer   0.5

0   Mile   0.5

N

To Sisters

242

P 27

Lava Camp
Trail #4060

Pacific Crest Trail

0.2

Pacific Crest Trail #2000

0.9/5.3

North Matthieu Lake Trail #4062

2.1

North
Matthieu
Lake

3.1

South
Matthieu
Lake

28 Whychus Creek

This hike takes you along the banks of scenic Whychus Creek past waterfalls and big rock pools in a gorgeous ponderosa pine forest.

Start: Whychus Creek trailhead off Three Creek Road (FR 16)
Distance: 6.8-mile out-and-back
Hiking time: 3 to 4 hours
Difficulty: Moderate due to some hills and trail length
Trail surface: Dirt path
Best season: Year-round; snow may be present during the winter months
Other trail users: None

Canine compatibility: Leashed dogs permitted
Land status: Deschutes National Forest
Nearest town: Sisters
Fees and permits: None
Schedule: Open all hours
Maps: USGS North Sister
Trail contact: Deschutes National Forest, Sisters Ranger District, 201 N. Pine St. and Hwy. 20, Sisters; (541) 549-7700; www.fs.usda.gov/main/deschutes/home

Finding the trailhead: From US 20 in downtown Sisters, turn south onto Elm Street. Travel 4.1 miles on Elm Street, which turns into Three Creek Road (FR 16), to a turnoff on the right side of the road marked by a brown hiker symbol. GPS: N44 14.116' / W121 33.71'

The Hike

This trail travels parallel to the scenic, 41-mile-long Whychus Creek. The name Whychus (pronounced why-choose) is derived from the Sahaptin language and means "the place we cross the water." The source of the creek is at the base of the Three Sisters Mountains, and it flows through the Deschutes Basin until it joins the Deschutes River near Lake Billy Chinook.

The route follows the picturesque creek through large stands of stately ponderosa pine trees. The creek has a character of its own due to its many scenic, geologic features created by glacial and volcanic events. As you hike the trail you will see numerous small waterfalls, a variety of channel shapes, giant boulders, rock spires, and channel beds of polished rock with potholes. At 0.2 mile you will pass by an old irrigation canal and canal switch that diverted the water from the creek for irrigation. After 1.8 miles the trail descends a rocky embankment and then continues to parallel the creek. At 2.2 miles you'll pass a nice viewpoint of a small waterfall. After 3.1 miles you'll arrive at the junction with the Metolius-Windigo Trail. This trail is popular with horseback riders. After the trail junction you'll pass a campground on the left that is sheltered by the canopy of beautiful old ponderosa pine trees. Continue left on the Whychus Creek Trail until it ends at 3.4 miles. This is your turnaround point; retrace the same route back to the trailhead.

Lovely Whychus Creek offers waterfalls and other scenic geologic features.

Miles and Directions

0.0   Start hiking on the signed trail that indicates "Metolius Windigo Trail 2¾, 800 Road Trail-head 3 Miles."

0.2   Pass an old irrigation canal and canal switch that once was used for irrigation.

1.8   Walk down a rocky hillside.

2.2   Arrive at a nice viewpoint of a small waterfall.

3.1   Arrive at a trail junction. Turn left. (The Metolius-Windigo Trail goes right.) You will pass by a campground on the left.

3.4   The trail ends. Retrace the same route back to the trailhead.

6.8   Arrive back at the trailhead.

Ken Skeen hiking with Tiz and Bear on the Whychus Creek Trail.

Hike Information

Local Information: Sisters Area Chamber of Commerce, 291 E. Main Ave., Sisters; (541) 549-0251 ; sisterscountry.com

Local Events and Attractions: Sisters Rodeo and Parade, second weekend in June, Sisters; (541) 549-0121; sistersrodeo.com

Sisters Folk Festival, late Sept, Sisters; (541) 549-4979; sistersfolkfestival.org

Restaurants: Sisters Coffee Company, 273 W. Hood Ave., Sisters; (541) 549-0527; sisterscoffee.com

Sisters Bakery, 251 E. Cascade, Sisters; (541) 549-0361; sistersbakery.com

Three Creeks Brewing, 721 S. Desperado Ct., Sisters; (541) 549-1963; three creeksbrewing.com

Whychus Creek

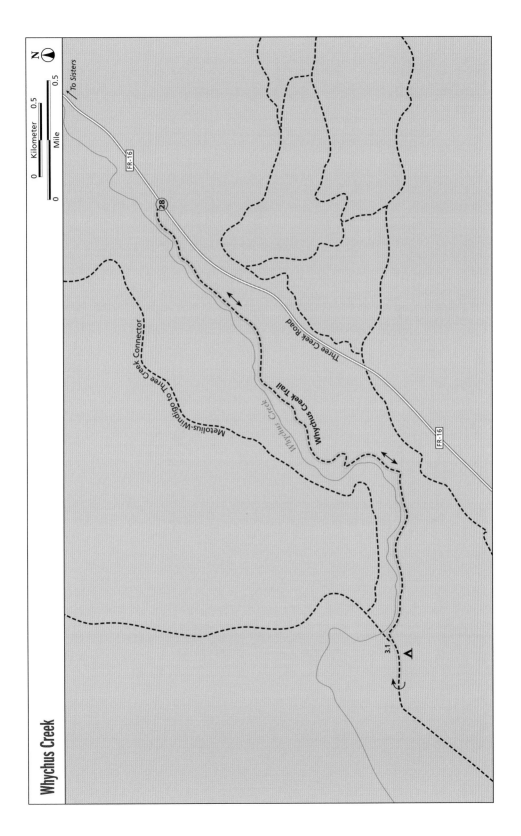

N

0   Kilometer   0.5

0   Mile   0.5

To Sisters

FR-16

28

Three Creek Road

Whychus Creek Trail

Whychus Creek

Metolius-Windigo to Three Creek Connector

FR-16

3.1

29 Whychus Canyon Preserve

This hike takes you on a tour of the scenic Whychus Canyon Preserve, which has many viewpoints of the Three Sisters and other Cascade peaks and Whychus Canyon. There are also options to explore other trails in this preserve, including a route that follows part of the historic Santiam Wagon Road.

Start: Whychus Canyon Preserve trailhead off Goodrich Road
Distance: 5.3-mile loop
Hiking time: 2.5 to 3 hours
Difficulty: Moderate due to some elevation gain and trail length
Trail surface: Dirt path
Best season: Apr through Oct
Other trail users: None
Canine compatibility: Leashed dogs permitted

Land status: Whychus Canyon Preserve
Nearest town: Sisters
Fees and permits: No fees or permits required
Schedule: Open all hours
Maps: Whychus Canyon Preserve Trail Map (available at the trailhead)
Trail contact: Deschutes Land Trust, 210 NW Irving, Ste. 102, Bend; (541) 330-0017; www. deschuteslandtrust.org

Finding the trailhead:

From Sisters:

Turn east from Sisters on OR 126 for approximately 5.4 miles. Turn left onto Goodrich Road. Follow Goodrich Road for 1.5 miles until the paved road begins to curve sharply to the right. Continue straight at the curve onto a gravel road and follow this road 1.3 miles north to a split in the road. You'll see the Whychus Canyon Preserve welcome sign straight ahead. Continue north for another 0.4 mile to the kiosk and parking area.

From OR 126 (Redmond, Madras, Prineville):

Turn right onto Goodrich Road. Follow Goodrich Road for 1.5 miles until the paved road begins to curve sharply to the right. Continue straight at the curve onto a gravel road and follow this road 1.3 miles north to a split in the road. You'll see the Whychus Canyon Preserve welcome sign straight ahead. Continue north for another 0.4 mile to the kiosk and parking area.

From US 20 (Bend, La Pine, Sunriver):

Take US 20 toward Sisters for approximately 13 miles. Turn right on Fryrear Road and continue 5.5 miles to the intersection with OR 126. Turn left onto OR 126 for 1 mile, then right onto Goodrich Road. Follow Goodrich Road for 1.5 miles until the paved road begins to curve sharply to the right. Continue straight at the curve onto a gravel road and follow this road 1.3 miles north to a split in the road. You'll see the Whychus Canyon Preserve welcome sign straight ahead. Continue north for another 0.4 mile to the kiosk and parking area.

The Hike

This route takes you on a tour of the Whychus Canyon Preserve outside Sisters. This 930-acre preserve on Whychus Creek was first established in 2010, and an

You will have nice views of the Whychus Creek Canyon from the Rim Trail.

additional 480 acres was added in 2014. The preserve contains over 7 miles of trails and offers scenic canyon views of Whychus Creek and Whychus Creek Canyon. The preserve is filled with grasslands, old-growth juniper, cottonwood, aspen stands, and colorful wildflowers. In addition to the route described here, you have multiple options for exploring different parts of the preserve. The Wagon Road and Meadow Loop Trail follow a section of the Santiam Wagon Road and have interpretive signs that tell the history of how it was used to settle Central Oregon.

The Santiam Wagon Road was built in the 1860s and served as a route from the Willamette Valley, across the Central Cascades, and through eastern Oregon to the Idaho border. It was almost 400 miles long and served as a freight and livestock route from 1865 to 1939. Many settlers in the Willamette Valley used the road to move their livestock east to Central Oregon to graze on the abundant grasses there. Those traveling west on the route were often in large wagon trains filled with wool. They traveled from Shaniko with wool to be processed in the woolen mills in the mid–Willamette Valley. Ranchers also traveled west to stock up on fruits and vegetables for the winter.

This route travels along the canyon rim, drops down into the canyon and follows the creek, loops back to the top of the canyon rim, and then leads back to your starting point. Along the way, you have many scenic viewpoints of the canyon and Central Cascades.

Miles and Directions

0.0 Start hiking where the trail sign Indicates "Rim and Creek Trails."
0.1 Go through a metal gate and then at the T intersection go right on the Rim Trail.
0.6 At the T intersection turn right and continue hiking on the Rim Trail.
1.4 Arrive at a rest bench and a nice viewpoint of the Whychus Creek Canyon. From the viewpoint, the trail descends through a large rock garden.
1.5 Arrive at a signed trail junction. Turn right on the Meadow and Wagon Road Trails.
1.6 At the signed trail junction turn left toward "Scenic Overlook–Rim and Creek Trails."
1.7 Go left at the signed trail junction toward Scenic Overlook. Follow the trail through a series of rocks to a scenic viewpoint of North Sister and the creek canyon. After enjoying the view return to the main trail and turn left.
3.0 Arrive at a T intersection. Stay right (straight) and continue on the signed Creek Trail.
4.1 Arrive at a T intersection. Turn right on the signed Rim Trail.
5.2 At the trail junction turn right and go through the gate.
5.3 Arrive back at the trailhead.

Hike Information

Local Information: Sisters Area Chamber of Commerce, 291 E. Main Ave., Sisters; (541) 549-0251; sisterscountry.com

Local Events and Attractions: Sisters Rodeo and Parade, second weekend in June, Sisters; (541) 549-0121; sistersrodeo.com

Sisters Folk Festival, late Sept, Sisters; (541) 549-4979; sistersfolkfestival.org

Restaurants: Sisters Coffee Company, 273 W. Hood Ave., Sisters; (541) 549-0527; sisterscoffee.com

Sisters Bakery, 251 E. Cascade, Sisters; (541) 549-0361; sistersbakery.com

Three Creeks Brewing, 721 S. Desperado Ct., Sisters; (541) 549-1963; threecreeksbrewing.com

Whychus Canyon Preserve

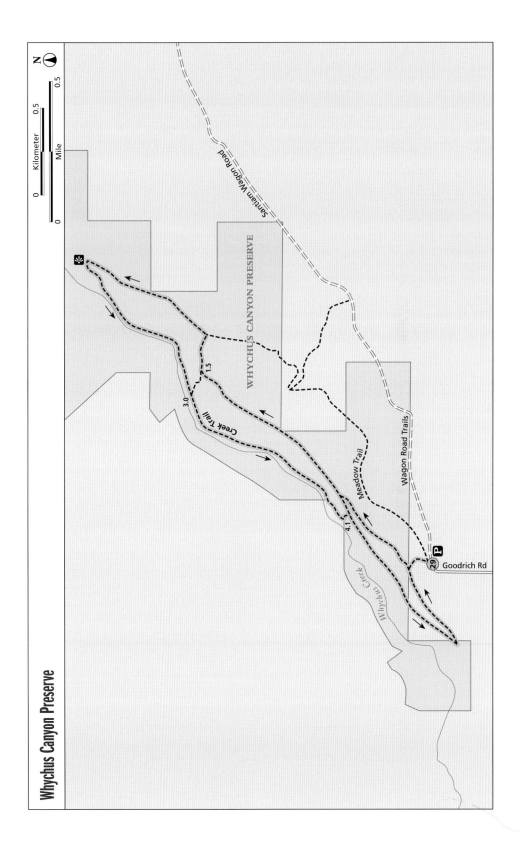

WHYCHUS CANYON PRESERVE

Santiam Wagon Road

Creek Trail

Meadow Trail

Wagon Road Trails

Whychus Creek

Goodrich Rd

29

3.0

1.5

4.1

N

Kilometer

Mile

0   0.5

0   0.5

30 Tam McArthur Rim

Located south of Sisters and east of Broken Top, Tam McArthur Rim is a wind-swept ridge offering outstanding views of Three Sisters country. On this hike, you will also enjoy dramatic views of the Three Creek Basin and the Central Cascade peaks.

Start: Tam McArthur Rim Trail 4078 trailhead off Three Creek Road (FR 16)

Distance: 5.0-mile out-and-back

Hiking time: 2.5 to 3.5 hours

Difficulty: Difficult due to steep ascent on multiple switchbacks

Trail surface: Dirt path

Best season: Late June through Oct; snow may be present through July

Other trail users: Horseback riders

Canine compatibility: Leashed dogs permitted

Land status: Deschutes National Forest and Three Sisters Wilderness

Nearest town: Sisters

Fees and permits: A Central Cascades Wilderness permit is required. You can reserve one by going to Recreation.gov. It is recommended to reserve your permit 2 days before you decide to go on your hike. Same-day permits may be available depending on how many people have reserved a permit.

Schedule: Open all hours

Maps: USGS Tumalo Falls and Broken Top

Trail contact: Deschutes National Forest, Sisters Ranger District, 201 N. Pine St. and Hwy. 20, Sisters; (541) 549-7700; www.fs.usda.gov/main/deschutes/home

Finding the trailhead: From US 20 in downtown Sisters, turn south onto Elm Street, which turns into Three Creek Road (FR 16). Head 15.6 miles south (the road becomes gravel after 14 miles) until you reach a sign for Driftwood Campground and turn right. Travel a short distance and park in the parking area on the right. GPS: N44 06.064' / W121 37.250'

The Hike

The Tam McArthur Rim Trail begins adjacent to Three Creek Lake, which resides in a basin carved by ice age glaciers and is a popular summer recreation spot for those living and visiting Central Oregon. It's stocked with rainbow and brook trout raised at the Wizard Falls Fish Hatchery northwest of Sisters. To the west of Three Creek Lake is Little Three Creek Lake, which can be reached via a 2.2-mile round-trip trail from Driftwood Campground.

Tam McArthur Rim takes its name from Lewis A. "Tam" McArthur, original author of *Oregon Geographic Names*. Interest in Oregon ran deep in the McArthur family. Both of Tam's grandfathers were involved in surveying Oregon and in Oregon politics. Born in The Dalles, Oregon, on April 27, 1883, McArthur worked for the Pacific Power & Light Company from 1923 to 1946. He also served as secretary to the Oregon Geographic Board from 1914 to 1949. It was during this time that

Nice view of Three Creek Lake and Tam McArthur Rim.

the idea of writing a book about Oregon's geographic names took shape. The first edition of *Oregon Geographic Names* was published in 1928. Today the book is in its sixth edition and is edited by McArthur's son, Lewis L. McArthur. After McArthur passed away in 1951, Robert W. Sawyer, a good friend of McArthur, named the prominent ridge above Three Creek Lake in his honor.

Begin this hike by heading south on steep switchbacks through a fir forest lined with grassy meadows and purple lupine. As the trail climbs, there are many opportunities to view the Three Creek Lake basin to the west. When the path reaches the ridge crest, at mile 1.8, it forks. At this point the landscape is wide open, with occasional groups of tough whitebark pines. The views are endless. Go right at the intersection and hike through a large open basin to a high point on the ridge. From there you can enjoy spectacular views of the Three Creek Lake basin to the east, the Three Sisters Mountains and Broken Top to the west, Mount Washington and Mount Jefferson to the northwest, and Mount Bachelor to the south. From here,

A bright bunch of late season wildflowers along the trail.

follow the same route back to the trailhead. Note there can be mosquitoes in the early summer months, and snow may be present through mid-July.

Miles and Directions

0.0　From the parking area, hike toward the main road. Cross the road and start hiking on a steep uphill at the wooden trailhead sign for Tam McArthur Rim Trail #4078. The sign indicates that it is 2.5 miles to the summit viewpoint. The trail climbs steeply the first 0.8 mile through a high alpine forest where open meadows, old tree logs, and bright purple lupine line the trail.

1.8　Turn right at the trail junction. Continue to the right on the Tam McArthur Rim Trail #4078 (the Tam McArthur Horse Trail #4078.1 goes left).

2.5　Arrive at a spectacular viewpoint. From this gorgeous vantage point, you'll have views of the Three Creek Lake basin to the east, Broken Top and the Three Sisters Mountains to the west, Mount Washington and Mount Jefferson to the northwest, and Mount Bachelor to the south. After enjoying the mesmerizing view, head back on the same route to your starting point.

5.0　Arrive back at the trailhead.

Hike Information

Local Information: Sisters Area Chamber of Commerce, 291 E. Main Ave., Sisters; (541) 549-0251; sisterscountry.com

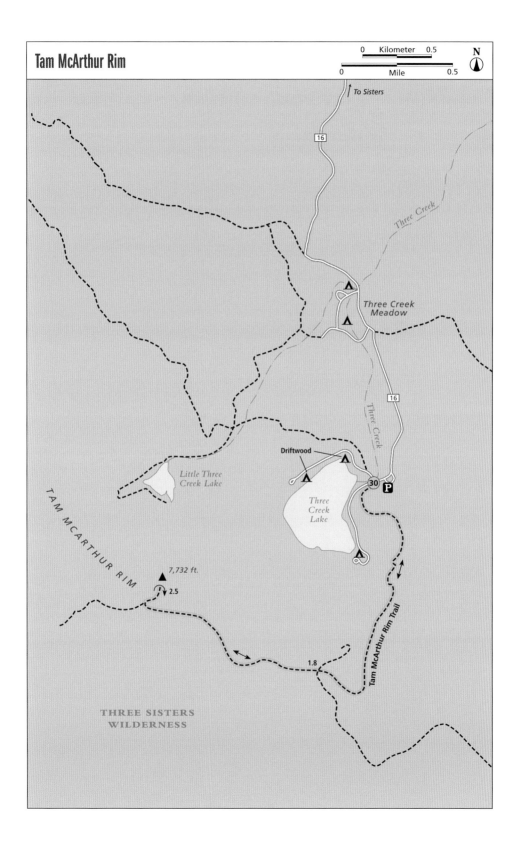

Tam McArthur Rim

0   Kilometer   0.5

0   Mile   0.5

N

↑ To Sisters

16

Three Creek

Three Creek
Meadow

16

Three Creek

Driftwood

30

P

Little Three
Creek Lake

Three
Creek
Lake

TAM MCARTHUR RIM

7,732 ft.

2.5

1.8

Tam McArthur Rim Trail

THREE SISTERS
WILDERNESS

Ken Skeen and Rahul Ravel enjoying the views.

Local Events and Attractions: Sisters Rodeo and Parade, second weekend in June, Sisters; (541) 549-0121; sistersrodeo.com

Sisters Folk Festival, late Sept, Sisters; (541) 549-4979; sistersfolkfestival.org

Restaurants: Sisters Coffee Company, 273 W. Hood Ave., Sisters; (541) 549-0527; sisterscoffee.com

Sisters Bakery, 251 E. Cascade, Sisters; (541) 549-0361; sistersbakery.com

Three Creeks Brewing, 721 S. Desperado Ct., Sisters; (541) 549-1963; three creeksbrewing.com

TRAIL TIPS

- This trail is popular among horseback riders.
- If you encounter a horse, step off the trail and give it room to pass. If you can, sit down. The less imposing you appear, the less likely you are to spook a horse.
- Bring mosquito repellent with you on this hike. There are plenty of hungry mosquitoes waiting for a good meal from unsuspecting hikers.

31 Smith Rock State Park

This scenic loop explores the volcanic landscapes of Smith Rock State Park. This world-class climbing area is packed with challenging multipitch routes, miles of hiking trails, and gorgeous scenery. This route takes you into a scenic river canyon carved by the Crooked River and then ascends to the top of Staender Ridge, where you'll have outstanding views of the Central Cascade peaks and the surrounding Central Oregon farmland and high desert. You will then descend back into the river canyon and have nice views of the Crooked River and the amazing rock spire called Monkey Face.

Start: Smith Rock State Park
Distance: 7.8-mile loop
Hiking time: 3.5 to 4.5 hours
Difficulty: Difficult due to steep ascent to the summit of Staender Ridge
Trail surface: Paved path, doubletrack road, and dirt path
Best season: Year-round
Other trail users: Mountain bikers, trail runners, and horseback riders
Canine compatibility: Leashed dogs permitted. However, this trail is not recommended for dogs during July and Aug due to extreme heat.
Land status: State park
Nearest town: Terrebonne
Fees and permits: A day-use parking pass is required and can be obtained at the self-pay station at the park.
Schedule: Open all hours
Maps: USGS Redmond
Trail contact: Oregon State Parks and Recreation, 725 Summer St. NE, Ste. C, Salem; (800) 551-6949; https://stateparks.oregon.gov

Finding the trailhead: From Redmond travel 5 miles north on US 97 to the small town of Terrebonne. At the flashing yellow light, turn right onto B Avenue (this becomes Smith Rock Way after the first stop sign). Continue 3.3 miles northeast following the signs to Smith Rock State Park. GPS: N44 21.894' / W121 08.287'

The Hike

Smith Rock is one of Central Oregon's most popular state parks. As you start the hike, you'll enjoy spectacular views of the park's colorful 400-foot-tall cliffs. These volcanic masterpieces started to take shape in the Miocene period, 17 to 19 million years ago, when hot steam and ash spewed from the ground. Traces of basalt can be found from the Newberry Volcano eruption 1.2 million years ago that formed Paulina and East Lakes. Since this volcanic activity the Crooked River has eroded the rock to form the columnar shapes that you see in the upper gorge today.

This 7.8-mile loop route begins from the main parking area and takes you past a shady picnic area with restrooms. You then begin a steep descent to the

You can enjoy far-reaching views of Smith Rock State Park and the Three Sisters Mountains from the summit of Staender Ridge.

canyon floor. A maintained viewpoint and interpretive sign along the way is an excellent place to take photos and to learn more about the park's geologic history.

If you have your canine partner with you, please be aware that during the hot summer months of July and August this route is not recommended because the ground can become very hot and burn your dog's feet. In addition, be aware that during this time you may see rattlesnakes. If you are hiking with your dog during the hot summer months, be sure you have foot protection for him or her. A cheap alternative to buying dog boots is to bring along a roll of Vetwrap, which is a stretchy gauze material that you can wrap your dog's paws with in the event he or she has a foot injury.

Once you reach the canyon floor, you will cross the Crooked River on a wood footbridge and then turn right onto the Wolf Tree Trail. This trail parallels the

Monkey Face is a popular climbing route in Smith Rock State Park.

Crooked River and winds through the scenic river canyon that is surrounded by stunning rock spires. Along this stretch of the trail watch for Canada geese, whose striking white throat patch and black head and neck make them easy to spot. The geese feed on the riverside vegetation and are apt to honk in alarm as you approach. Also keep an eye out for river otters, which are sometimes seen along this stretch of the river.

After 1.4 miles you'll turn left and start climbing steeply uphill on the Burma Road Trail. The Burma Road Trail ascends steeply over the next 1.1 miles to the spectacular summit of Staender Ridge. Be sure to take a break and soak in the views of the Three Sisters, Broken Top, and other Central Cascade peaks as well as the amazing rock spires of Smith Rock. From the summit you will hook up with the Summit Loop Trail, which descends for a few miles along the northern edge of the park to the junction with the River Trail. Follow the River Trail as it parallels the Crooked River over the next 2.4 miles. Along the way there are some good swimming holes with small sandy beaches that are worth checking out. Finish the loop by crossing the wood footbridge and making the short, steep climb back to your starting point.

Miles and Directions

0.0 From the parking area, follow the paved trail as it parallels the canyon rim.

0.2 Turn left onto the wide path that descends into the canyon. Go a short distance and turn right onto The Chute Trail.

0.4 Pass a drinking fountain and rest area on the right, then cross a wood footbridge over the Crooked River. After crossing the bridge, turn right onto the Wolf Tree Trail.

1.4 At the trail junction turn left and start hiking uphill. After about 50 feet turn left onto the signed Burma Road Trail. (**Note:** If you go right, the trail heads toward the Student Wall—a climbing area that is popular with beginning climbers.)

1.6 Turn left onto the signed Burma Road Trail.

2.5 Arrive at the top of Staender Ridge. Take a break and soak in the gorgeous views. At the junction with the Summit Loop Trail, turn left and start descending.

4.0 Arrive at the junction with the signed Summit Loop Viewpoint. Go right and continue hiking on the Summit Loop Trail. After another 0.5 mile you'll have great views of Monkey Face—a stunning 350-foot rock with multiple climbing routes and a cave that mimics a monkey's mouth.

5.0 Arrive at a junction with the Mesa Verde Trail. Continue straight (right) and follow the River Trail as it parallels the Crooked River.

7.4 Turn right and cross the wood footbridge. Follow the trail until it intersects with The Chute Trail. Turn left onto The Chute Trail and follow it until you reach the canyon rim.

7.6 Turn right onto the path that follows the canyon rim.

7.8 Arrive back at the main parking area and your starting point.

Hike Information

Local Information: Redmond Chamber of Commerce, 446 SW 7th St., Redmond; (541) 923-5191; visitredmondoregon.com

Redpoint Climber's Supply, 8222 US 97, #101, Terrebonne; (541) 604-2115; redpointclimbing.com

Restaurants: Terrebonne Depot, 400 NW Smith Rock Way, Terrebonne; (541) 527-4339; www.terrebonnedepotrestaurant.com

PEREGRINE FALCONS

Peregrines are the high-speed flyers of the raptor world. With their sharp, pointed wings they can dive up to 275 miles per hour. In addition to their stunning speed and agility, peregrines have remarkably keen eyes. Their eyesight is eight times sharper than ours, and two times that of a golden eagle's. They can spot a bird up to 5 miles away. Peregrines feed primarily off small- to medium-size birds, which they carefully pick from the air. The flocks of pigeons that nest in the park are a favorite meal of the resident clan of peregrines.

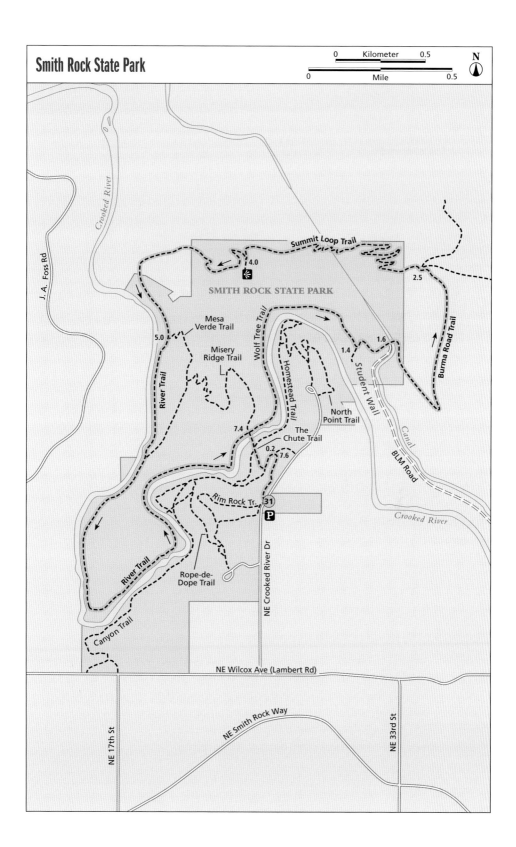

Smith Rock State Park

0 Kilometer 0.5

0 Mile 0.5

N

Crooked River

J. A. Foss Rd

Summit Loop Trail

4.0

2.5

SMITH ROCK STATE PARK

Mesa Verde Trail

5.0

Misery Ridge Trail

Wolf Tree Trail

Homestead Trail

1.4   1.6

River Trail

Student Wall

Burma Road Trail

North Point Trail

Canal

7.4

The Chute Trail

BLM Road

0.2   7.6

Rim Rock Tr.   31

P

Crooked River

River Trail

Rope-de-Dope Trail

Canyon Trail

NE Crooked River Dr

NE Wilcox Ave (Lambert Rd)

NE 17th St

NE Smith Rock Way

NE 33rd St

32 Gray Butte

This route travels through a fragrant sage and juniper landscape of the Crooked River National Grassland. At the trail's turnaround point, you'll have grand views of the Central Cascade Mountains. An optional shuttle route takes you to Smith Rock State Park.

Start: Gray Butte Trail trailhead in Crooked River National Grassland
Distance: 3.8-mile out-and-back
Hiking time: 2 to 3 hours
Difficulty: Easy due to well-graded trail
Trail surface: Dirt path
Best season: Year-round
Other trail users: Horseback riders and mountain bikers
Canine compatibility: Dogs permitted

Land status: National grassland
Nearest town: Terrebonne
Fees and permits: None
Schedule: Open all hours
Maps: USGS Gray Butte
Trail contact: Crooked River National Grassland, 274 SW 4th St., Madras; (541) 416-6640; www.fs.usda.gov/recarea/ochoco/recarea/?recid=38274

Finding the trailhead: *From Redmond:* Travel 5 miles north on US 97 to the small town of Terrebonne. At the flashing yellow light, turn right onto B Avenue (Smith Rock Way). Go 4.7 miles and turn left (north) onto Lone Pine Road. Continue 4.4 miles to the junction with FR 5710. Turn left onto FR 5710 (you'll pass Skull Hollow Campground on your left). Follow FR 5710 as it winds up Skull Hollow Canyon for 2.6 miles. Turn left onto FR 57 and continue 0.6 mile to a gravel pullout on the left side of the road.
From Madras: From the junction of US 97 and US 26 in Madras, travel south on US 26 for 13.6 miles. Turn right onto Lone Pine Road and continue 3.2 miles, then turn right onto FR 5710 (you'll pass Skull Hollow Campground on your left). Follow FR 5710 as it winds up Skull Hollow Canyon for 2.6 miles. Turn left onto FR 57 and continue 0.6 mile to a gravel pullout on the left side of the road.
GPS: N44 23.974' / W121 5.891'

The Hike

The Gray Butte Trail travels along the west side of Gray Butte through an open grassland filled with fragrant sagebrush and juniper trees. This prominent butte rises 5,108 feet above the Central Oregon high desert and is part of a series of rounded buttes that provide a unique texture to the landscape. Gray Butte is part of the Crooked River National Grassland, established in 1960.

As you hike this trail, you may see range cows that are allowed to graze in this area during certain times of the year. This trail is also open to mountain bikers, and they can often be seen riding on this trail.

After following the singletrack trail for 1.9 miles, you'll arrive at a side trail on the right that leads to the Austin Creson Viewpoint. A memorial plaque for Austin Creson is located at this point and is dedicated to his hard work on planning the

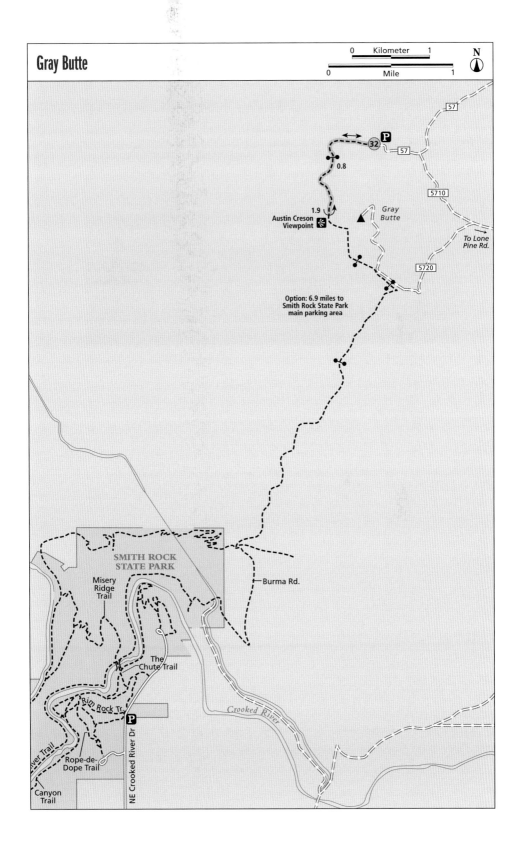

Gray Butte

0   Kilometer   1

0   Mile   1

N

57

32

P

57

5710

0.8

1.9

Austin Creson
Viewpoint

Gray
Butte

To Lone
Pine Rd.

5720

Option: 6.9 miles to
Smith Rock State Park
main parking area

SMITH ROCK
STATE PARK

Misery
Ridge
Trail

The
Chute Trail

Burma Rd.

Bim Rock Tr.

P

Crooked River

River Trail

Rope-de-
Dope Trail

Canyon
Trail

NE Crooked River Dr

Mount Jefferson.

Gray Butte Trail. From the viewpoint you'll have a spectacular view of the Three Sisters Mountains, Broken Top, Black Butte, and Mount Jefferson. After enjoying the views, retrace the same route back to the trailhead.

Miles and Directions

0.0 Start hiking on the signed Gray Butte Trail.
0.8 Go through a green metal gate.
1.9 Turn right onto a side trail that leads to the Austin Creson Viewpoint. After enjoying the views, retrace the same route back to the trailhead.
3.8 Arrive back at the trailhead.

Option

Continue 6.9 miles to the Smith Rock State Park main parking area. You can leave a car at Smith Rock and complete this as an 8.8-mile shuttle hike.

Hike Information

Local Information: Redmond Chamber of Commerce, 446 SW 7th St., Redmond; (541) 923-5191; visitredmondoregon.com

Redpoint Climber's Supply, 8222 US 97, #101, Terrebonne; (541) 604-2115; redpointclimbing.com

Restaurants: Terrebonne Depot, 400 NW Smith Rock Way, Terrebonne; (541) 527-4339; www.terrebonnedepotrestaurant.com

Cascade Lakes Brewery, 855 SW 7th St., Redmond; (541) 923-1795; cascade lakes.com

33 Rimrock Springs Natural Area

This easy hike takes you on a tour of the fragrant juniper and sagebrush landscape of the Rimrock Springs Natural Area. This wildlife area features a productive marsh where you can see geese, ducks, and other wildlife from two viewing platforms along the route. This hike also features interpretive signs in English and Spanish, and the first 0.5 mile of the trail is paved.

Start: Rimrock Springs Wildlife Management Area parking area
Distance: 1.7-mile loop
Hiking time: About 1 hour
Difficulty: Easy due to well-graded trail
Trail surface: Paved path and dirt path
Best season: Year-round
Other trail users: None
Canine compatibility: Leashed dogs permitted

Land status: National grassland
Nearest town: Terrebonne
Fees and permits: None
Schedule: Open all hours
Maps: USGS Gray Butte
Trail contact: Crooked River National Grassland, 274 SW 4th St., Madras; (541) 416-6640; www.fs.usda.gov/recarea/ochoco/recarea/?recid=38274

Finding the trailhead: *From Redmond:* Travel 5 miles north on US 97 to the small town of Terrebonne. At the flashing yellow light, turn right onto B Avenue (Smith Rock Way). Go 4.7 miles and turn left (north) onto Lone Pine Road. Continue 7.2 miles to the intersection with US 26. Turn left onto US 26 and go 4.4 miles to the parking area signed Rimrock Springs Wildlife Management Area, located on the right side of the highway.
From Madras: Drive south on US 97 for 2 miles to a sign that indicates Prineville/Mitchell/John Day. Turn left (east) onto US 26. Travel 8.5 miles south to the Rimrock Springs parking area on the left side of the highway. GPS: N44 29.728' / W121 03.361'

The Hike

This short hike travels through a sagebrush and juniper landscape in the Rimrock Springs Natural Area located in the Crooked River National Grassland. You'll start the hike by walking on a paved path for 0.5 mile to a side trail that leads to a wood viewing platform. From the platform you'll have nice views of a productive cattail marsh. Look for ducks, geese, and raptors.

After enjoying the view, continue on the main trail. In the spring months look for the striking lupine wildflower, which has purple-bluish blossoms and silvery-green leaves. You may also see jackrabbits hopping through the sagebrush and small groups of quail. At 0.7 mile turn left onto a side trail that leads to another viewing platform. Return to the main trail as it climbs to the top of a small rise and takes you next to some jumbled lava outcroppings. At 1.2 miles turn left at a signed viewpoint where you have views of a wide valley and the Three Sisters Mountains with Mount

143

The author's dogs Tiz and Zane at a nice viewpoint of the Three Sisters Mountains.

Bachelor as a backdrop. After 1.6 miles the loop portion of the trail ends, and you'll follow the paved path back to the trailhead.

Miles and Directions

0.0 Start hiking on the paved path adjacent to the parking area.

0.1 The trail forks; go left.

0.5 Arrive at a trail junction (the paved path ends). Turn left and walk on a side trail to a viewing platform. Enjoy the views of the marsh and then return to the main trail. Back at the main trail, turn left and continue on the signed loop trail.

0.7 Turn left onto a side trail that leads to another viewing platform. After enjoying the views, return to the main trail and turn left to continue the loop.

1.2 Turn left at the signed viewpoint. Enjoy views of the Three Sisters and Mount Bachelor. After soaking in the views, return to the main loop trail and turn left.

1.6 The loop trail ends. Turn left onto the paved path.

1.7 Arrive back at the trailhead.

The author and her dogs Zane and Tiz on the viewing platform. Photo credit: Ken Skeen

Hike Information

Local Information: Redmond Chamber of Commerce, 446 SW 7th St., Redmond; (541) 923-5191; visitredmondoregon.com

Redpoint Climber's Supply, 8222 US 97, #101, Terrebonne; (541) 604-2115; redpointclimbing.com

Restaurants: Terrebonne Depot, 400 NW Smith Rock Way, Terrebonne; (541) 527-4339; www.terrebonnedepotrestaurant.com

Cascade Lakes Brewery, 855 SW 7th St., Redmond; (541) 923-1795; cascadelakes .com

Ken Skeen stops for a break in the Rimrock Springs Natural Area.

WESTERN RATTLESNAKE

The only venomous snake in the Pacific Northwest is the western rattlesnake. These snakes are 2 to 4 feet in length, have a diamond-shaped head, and are brown, with large rounded blotches on their back and black-and-white crossbars on the tail. A rattle is also present on the tail. Western rattlesnakes prefer dry, sunny locations near rock piles, cliffs, or downed logs. These snakes feed on mice, gophers, squirrels, and rabbits, but will also hunt birds, lizards, and amphibians. This snake will shake its rattle when it is startled or provoked, giving you a warning. Western rattlesnakes are not aggressive unless provoked. As with other wildlife, if you see a rattlesnake, you should respect it and leave it alone.

Rimrock Springs Natural Area

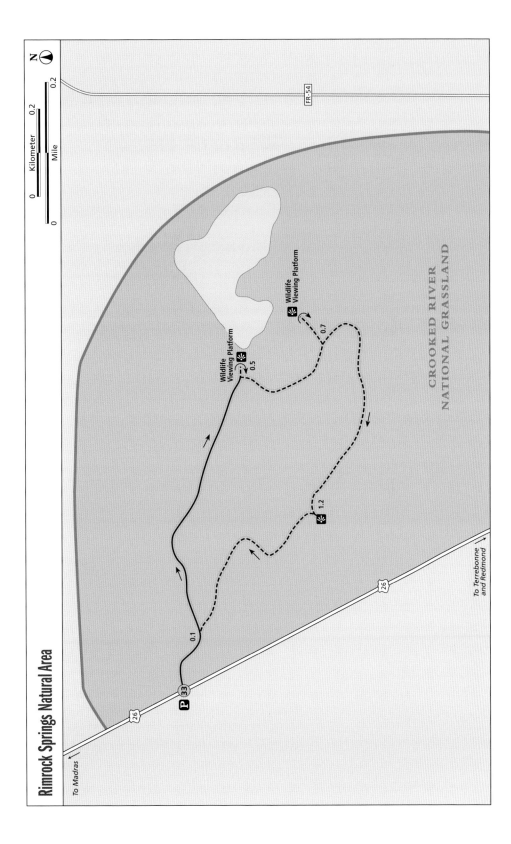

N

0   Kilometer   0.2
0   Mile   0.2

To Madras

26

P 33

26

To Terrebonne
and Redmond

0.1

Wildlife
Viewing Platform
0.5

Wildlife
Viewing Platform
0.7

1.2

CROOKED RIVER
NATIONAL GRASSLAND

FR-54

34 Tam-a-lau Trail

This loop trail takes you more than 600 feet to the top of a high peninsula above Lake Billy Chinook in Cove Palisades State Park. From there you have far-reaching views of the vast reservoir below and the snowcapped Central Cascade peaks, including Mount Hood, Mount Jefferson, Broken Top, Mount Bachelor, and the Three Sisters. The Crooked, Deschutes, and Metolius Rivers feed this giant lake, which is popular with boaters.

Start: Tam-a-lau Trailhead in Cove Palisades State Park

Distance: 6.8-mile lollipop loop

Hiking time: 3.5 to 4.5 hours

Difficulty: Moderate due to 600 feet of elevation gain to the top of The Peninsula

Trail surface: Paved path and dirt path

Best season: Sept through June

Other trail users: None

Canine compatibility: Leashed dogs permitted

Land status: State park

Nearest town: Madras

Fees and permits: A day-use parking pass is required and can be obtained at the self-pay station at the park.

Schedule: Dawn to dusk

Maps: USGS Round Butte Dam

Trail contact: Oregon State Parks and Recreation, 725 Summer St. NE, Ste. C, Salem; (800) 551-6949; https://stateparks.oregon.gov

Finding the trailhead: *From Redmond:* Travel 19 miles north on US 97 to a turnoff for Cove Palisades State Park and Culver/Round Butte Dam. Turn left (west) onto the Culver Highway and follow the state park signs for 6 miles to the park entrance. Follow the entrance road down into the canyon to a road junction. At the bottom of the canyon, turn left toward Deschutes Campground and day-use areas. Continue 3.7 miles to another road junction. Drive past the campground entrance and continue 0.25 mile to the signed Tam-a-lau parking area.
From Madras: Follow US 97 south and then follow signs approximately 15 miles southwest to the park. Once you reach the park entrance, follow the directions described above.
GPS: N44 3.461' / W121 17.334'

The Hike

This high desert hike gives you incredible views from the high rocky plateau called The Peninsula. The route climbs at a steady pace for a little over a mile to the top of a long, flat plateau. The hillside is blanketed with bunchgrass, yellow balsamroot, and purple lupine mixed with fragrant rabbitbrush and sagebrush.

After 1.6 miles you'll start the loop section of the hike, located on the top of The Peninsula. This plateau is made up of rock and sediment that were deposited by the Deschutes River over thousands of years. The sediment and rock are mixed with layers of basalt, a result of massive lava flows that covered this area from different

A spectacular view of Lake Billy Chinook.

eruptions of Cascade volcanoes. The lava flows filled the three river canyons carved by the Deschutes, Metolius, and Crooked Rivers, water sources for Lake Billy Chinook. Over thousands of years the rivers carved away the rock layers to produce the magnificent canyons that are present here today.

After 2.7 miles you'll arrive at a dramatic viewpoint and a great place to take a break and eat lunch. After 5.2 miles you'll end the loop and descend on the same route back to your starting point.

Avoid this hike during July and August when temperatures can hover in the 90s. If you're visiting during those months, explore the trail in the early morning when it is cooler, and be sure to bring plenty of water.

Miles and Directions

0.0 Start hiking toward the entrance to the parking area. On the left side of the road, at the brown hiker symbol, turn onto a hiking trail that parallels the road.

0.1 Cross a paved road and walk through an opening in a fence around Deschutes Campground A.

Zane taking a break.

0.5 Turn right onto a dirt path adjacent to a large interpretive sign. Over the next 1.1 miles, the trail ascends steeply to a high plateau above the lake.

1.4 Turn left onto a wide doubletrack road.

1.6 Turn left and begin the loop portion of the hike. Follow the dirt path as it parallels the edge of the rimrock and offers outstanding views of the lake canyon and the Central Cascade peaks.

2.7 Arrive at the tip of The Peninsula, which serves as a good lunch spot.

5.2 The loop portion of the hike ends. Descend on the same route back to your starting point.

6.8 Arrive back at the parking area.

Additional Hiking Options:

• Crooked River Rim Trail: This 2-mile out-and-back trail gives you nice views of the Cascade Mountains and the Crooked River Arm and distant views of the

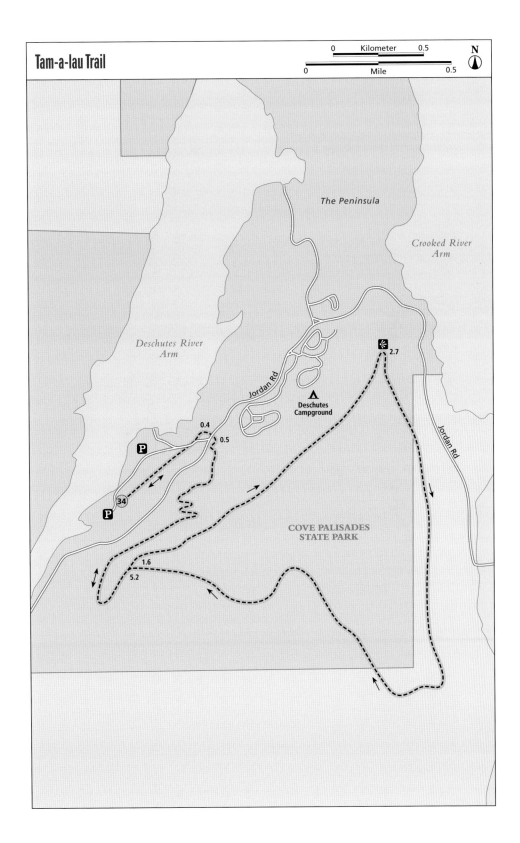

Tam-a-lau Trail

0   Kilometer   0.5

0   Mile   0.5

N

The Peninsula

Crooked River Arm

Deschutes River Arm

Jordan Rd

Deschutes Campground

0.4

0.5

P

34

P

2.7

Jordan Rd

1.6

5.2

COVE PALISADES STATE PARK

Lake Billy Chinook.

Deschutes Arm of Lake Billy Chinook Reservoir. This trail also provides great views of "The Island," a 200-acre landform that splits the two arms of the reservoir and provides a healthy habitat for raptors. You can access this trail adjacent to the Crooked River Campground.

- Wetland Nature Loop: This 0.25-mile trail allows you to potentially see rabbits, deer, and hawks. This area is also a monarch butterfly habitat and contains milk-weed, coyote willow, and red twig dogwood. You can access this trail adjacent to the Crooked River Campground.

Hike Information

Local Information: Madras Chamber of Commerce, 274 SW 4th St., Madras; (541) 475-2350; madraschamber.com

Restaurants: Madras Brewing, 212 SW 4th St., Ste. 104, Madras; (541) 316-6505; madrasbrewing.com

35 Steelhead Falls

This route takes you into the dramatic Deschutes River canyon to a viewpoint of Steelhead Falls. During the summer months this hike also has opportunities to cool off in the river.

Start: Steelhead Falls Trailhead in Crooked River Ranch
Distance: 2.8-mile out-and-back
Hiking time: 1.5 to 3 hours
Difficulty: Easy due to smooth trail surface
Trail surface: Dirt path
Best season: Year-round
Other trail users: None
Canine compatibility: Leashed dogs permitted

Land status: National grassland
Nearest town: Terrebonne
Fees and permits: None
Schedule: Open all hours
Maps: USGS Steelhead Falls
Trail contact: Bureau of Land Management, Prineville District Office, 3050 NE Third St., SW River Road, Prineville; (541) 416-6700; www. blm.gov/visit/steelhead-falls-trail

Finding the trailhead: From Redmond, travel 5 miles north on US 97 to the small town of Terrebonne. From Terrebonne continue another 0.5 mile north on US 97. Turn left onto Lower Bridge Way and proceed 2.1 miles. Turn right onto NW 43rd Street and travel 1.8 miles to a T junction. Turn left onto NW Chinook Drive and proceed 1 mile. Turn left onto Badger Road and drive for 1.7 miles. Turn right onto Quail Road and proceed 1.1 miles. Turn left onto River Road and continue 0.9 mile to the trailhead parking area. GPS: N44 24.677' / W121 17.559'

The Hike

This hike takes you into the Deschutes River canyon to a scenic view of Steelhead Falls. The hike is popular in the summer months with locals living in Crooked River Ranch, who like to fish and swim along this section of the Deschutes River.

Start hiking on the signed trail, which descends into the river canyon. At 0.1 mile the trail takes you to a nice viewpoint of the river canyon. At 0.5 mile you'll arrive at a viewpoint of Steelhead Falls. The short, broad waterfall is very dramatic as it plunges over a rocky ledge into a deep pool below. The area below the falls is popular for swimming. From the viewpoint of the falls, you can hike another mile along the river's edge. At 1.3 miles you will need to navigate through a large boulder field. At 1.4 miles you have nice views of the rock spires and pinnacles that tower above the river canyon, which are part of the Deschutes Formation.

Scenic Steelhead Falls.

REDMOND

Located 15 miles north of Bend on US 97, Redmond is a great starting point for many hikes in this guide. But you might want to start with Redmond itself. It was established in 1910 and has a historic downtown district that is worth exploring. The town is also home to Robert's Field—the region's only commercial airline service airport—and is also host to the Deschutes County Fair and Expo complex.

One of the premier hikes around Redmond is Smith Rock State Park. This park is located 8 miles northeast of Redmond off US 97 and promises scenic views of the Crooked River canyon and volcanic cliffs in the park. Smith Rock State Park is also a world-class climbing area, and you'll have many opportunities to watch climbers scaling the cliff faces.

Ken Skeen and Tiz enjoying the trail.

Another hike off the beaten path that offers a lot of solitude is Alder Springs. This 7.4-mile out-and-back hike takes you deep into a scenic creek canyon carved by Whychus Creek in the Crooked River National Grassland. The route offers spectacular canyon scenery and opportunities for swimming during the summer months.

Other hikes in the Crooked River National Grassland that offer a variety of views and are less crowded include Gray Butte and Rimrock Springs Natural Area.

The scenic Deschutes River canyon is popular for recreational activities.

Miles and Directions

0.0 Start hiking on the signed dirt path.
0.1 Pass a viewpoint of the river canyon.
0.5 Arrive at a viewpoint of Steelhead Falls.
1.3 Be careful as the trail passes through a large boulder field.
1.4 Arrive at the trail's end. Turn around and retrace the same route back to the trailhead.
2.8 Arrive back at the trailhead.

Hike Information

Local Information: Redmond Chamber of Commerce, 446 SW 7th St., Redmond; (541) 923-5191; visitredmondoregon.com

Redpoint Climber's Supply, 8222 US 97, #101, Terrebonne; (541) 604-2115; redpointclimbing.com

Restaurants: Terrebonne Depot, 400 NW Smith Rock Way, Terrebonne; (541) 527-4339; www.terrebonnedepotrestaurant.com

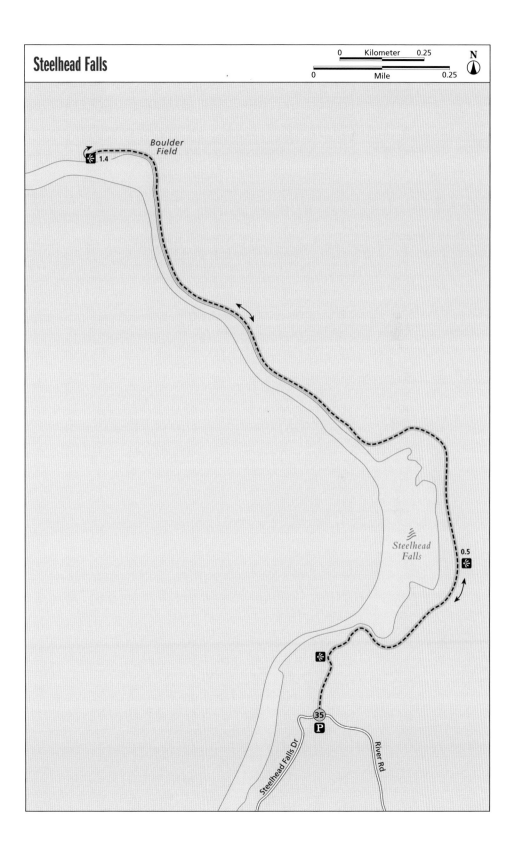

Steelhead Falls

0   Kilometer   0.25

0   Mile   0.25

N

Boulder
Field

1.4

Steelhead
Falls

0.5

35

P

Steelhead Falls Dr

River Rd

36 Alder Springs

This hidden gem is one of the best trails in the Crooked River National Grassland. It takes you into a dramatic canyon carved by Whychus Creek. Bubbling Whychus Creek is fed by several natural springs that you can view along the route. The trail parallels Whychus Creek and passes by some hidden camp spots shaded by towering ponderosa pine trees. The trail follows Whychus Creek until the turnaround point, where the creek joins up with the Deschutes River.

Start: Alder Springs Trailhead in Crooked River National Grassland
Distance: 7.4-mile out-and-back
Hiking time: 3 to 5 hours
Difficulty: Moderate due to creek crossing and elevation gain
Trail surface: Dirt path with a creek crossing
Best season: Year-round
Other trail users: None
Canine compatibility: Leashed dogs permitted

Land status: National grassland
Nearest town: Terrebonne
Fees and permits: None
Schedule: Open all hours
Maps: USGS Henkle Butte
Trail contact: Crooked River National Grassland, 274 SW 4th St., Madras; (541) 416-4660; www.fs.usda.gov/recarea/ochoco/recarea/?recid=38274

Finding the trailhead: From Redmond, travel 6.5 miles north on US 97, passing through the small town of Terrebonne. On the north end of Terrebonne, turn left onto Lower Bridge Way. Travel 16.9 miles on Lower Bridge Way, then turn left onto Holmes Road. Go 2.2 miles on Holmes Road and turn right onto FR 6360 (a dirt doubletrack road). Go through the green gate and continue 4 miles; turn right where a sign indicates "Alder Springs." Continue another 0.8 mile to the trailhead and parking area. GPS: N44 25.966' / W121 21.462'

The Hike

If you are seeking solitude with scenery and opportunities for swimming during the summer months, you will want to check out this hike. It is located in the Crooked River National Grassland and is enough off the beaten path that you will not see many other people. Use caution if you are hiking with your canine partner during the summer months. The canyon can be very hot, and the trail surface can heat up enough that it will burn the pads of your dog's feet. If you do want to hike on a hot day, be sure to bring foot protection for your dog.

You start hiking on the dirt path that descends into the Whychus Creek canyon over the next 1.3 miles. You'll have nice views of the Central Cascade Mountains as well as the impressive Deschutes Formation that exposes the multicolored layers of volcanic rock and eroded rock spires. You'll also see many of the natural springs

The author and her dog Tiz enjoying the canyon views. Photo credit: Ken Skeen

that feed Whychus Creek, bubbling out of the rocky ground. After 0.1 mile you will arrive at a signed trail junction for the Old Bridge Trail. (**Option:** To explore this spur trail, turn left and follow the trail 0.3 mile downhill to the junction with Whychus Creek.)

On the main trail, after 1.3 miles you will arrive at Whychus Creek and a crossing. (Bring extra shoes for this crossing.) The creek is lined with shaded grassy banks and abundant greenery. After crossing the creek follow the dirt path as it parallels the creek for another 2.4 miles. Along the way you'll pass many hidden campsites shaded by towering ponderosa pines that make excellent places to spend the night (as well as have great swimming spots) if you plan on backpacking into the canyon. The trail's turnaround point is where the creek joins the Deschutes River. Giant boulders and towering ponderosas make the

Ken Skeen admiring the rock formations on the route.

turnaround point a great place to take a break and enjoy views of the fast-flowing Deschutes River.

Miles and Directions

0.0   Start hiking on the dirt path.

0.1   The trail intersects with the signed Old Bridge Trail, which goes left. (**Side trip:** This trail continues 0.3 mile [one-way] downhill to its end at Whychus Creek.)

1.3   Arrive at Whychus Creek. Cross the creek and continue on the dirt path.

3.7   Arrive at the trail's turnaround point under towering ponderosa pine trees and large boulders next to the Deschutes River. Retrace the same route back to your starting point.

7.4   Arrive back at the trailhead.

Hike Information

Local Information: Redmond Chamber of Commerce, 446 SW 7th St., Redmond; (541) 923-5191; visitredmondoregon.com

Nice canyon views.

Redpoint Climber's Supply, 8222 US 97, #101, Terrebonne; (541) 604-2115; redpointclimbing.com

Restaurants: Terrebonne Depot, 400 NW Smith Rock Way, Terrebonne; (541) 527-4339; www.terrebonnedepotrestaurant.com

PRINEVILLE

The small town of Prineville is the gateway to the Ochoco National Forest and the Mill Creek Wilderness, both of which have many trails that offer more solitude than those closer to Bend. You can hike to the base of 350-foot Steins Pillar located in the Ochoco National Forest or to the base of Chimney Rock—another prominent rock formation located in the Crooked River National Grassland. The Twin Pillars Trail takes you through the quiet and scenic Mill

Deschutes River canyon.

Creek Wilderness along the banks of Mill Creek and then to the base of the Twin Pillars rock formation. Another recommended destination is the Painted Hills Unit of the John Day Fossil Beds National Monument, which is located about 52 miles northeast of Prineville off US 26. Several short hikes in this area feature close-up views of the area's fossil beds and beautifully colored hills.

GREEN TIP

Before you start for home, have you left the wilderness
as you'd want to see it?

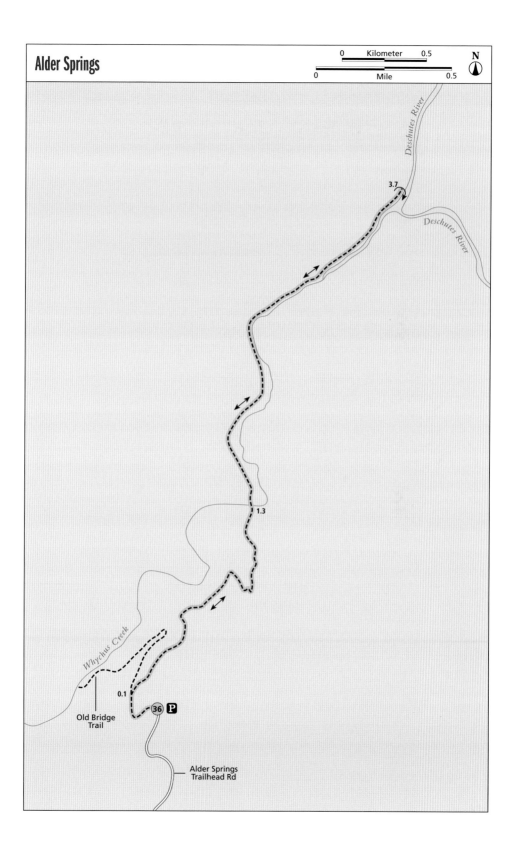

Alder Springs

0   Kilometer   0.5

0   Mile   0.5

N

Deschutes River

Deschutes River

3.7

1.3

Whychus Creek

0.1

Old Bridge
Trail

36   P

Alder Springs
Trailhead Rd

37 Chimney Rock

Chimney Rock is a prominent rock formation located high above the Crooked River. This short hike takes you on a tour through a high desert ecosystem of sage and juniper to the base of Chimney Rock, where you can enjoy views of the Crooked River canyon and the Central Cascade Mountains.

Start: Rim Trail trailhead across from Chimney Rock Recreation Area

Distance: 2.8-mile out-and-back

Hiking time: 1 to 1.5 hours

Difficulty: Moderate due to elevation gain to the base of Chimney Rock

Trail surface: Dirt path

Best season: Year-round

Other trail users: None

Canine compatibility: Leashed dogs permitted. However, this trail is not recommended for dogs during July and August due to extreme heat.

Land status: Bureau of Land Management

Nearest town: Prineville

Fees and permits: None

Schedule: Open all hours

Maps: USGS Stearns Butte

Trail contact: Bureau of Land Management, Prineville District, 3050 NE Third St., Prineville; (541) 416-6700; www.blm.gov/office/prineville-district-office

Finding the trailhead: From US 26 in downtown Prineville, turn south onto Main Street (OR 27). Continue south for 17.1 miles to a gravel parking area on the left side of the road marked "Rim Trail." The trailhead is located across from the Chimney Rock Recreation Area. GPS: N44 08.127' / W120 48.828'

The Hike

This short hike to the base of Chimney Rock gives you scenic views of the Crooked River canyon and the Central Cascade Mountains. From the trailhead you'll follow a series of switchbacks up a grass- and sage-covered hillside. As the trail climbs higher, you'll pass some twisted and gnarled juniper trees. Their stunted growth hides their age—some of the trees here are more than a century old. After 1.4 miles you'll arrive at the dramatic spire of Chimney Rock. Enjoy the views and then retrace the same route back to the trailhead. If you want to camp, you can stay in the Chimney Rock Recreation Area campground, which is located across from the trailhead. There are many prime campsites right next to the Crooked River.

Miles and Directions

0.0 Start hiking on the signed dirt path.

1.4 Arrive at the base of Chimney Rock and your turnaround point. Retrace the same route back to the trailhead.

2.8 Arrive back at the trailhead.

Chimney Rock

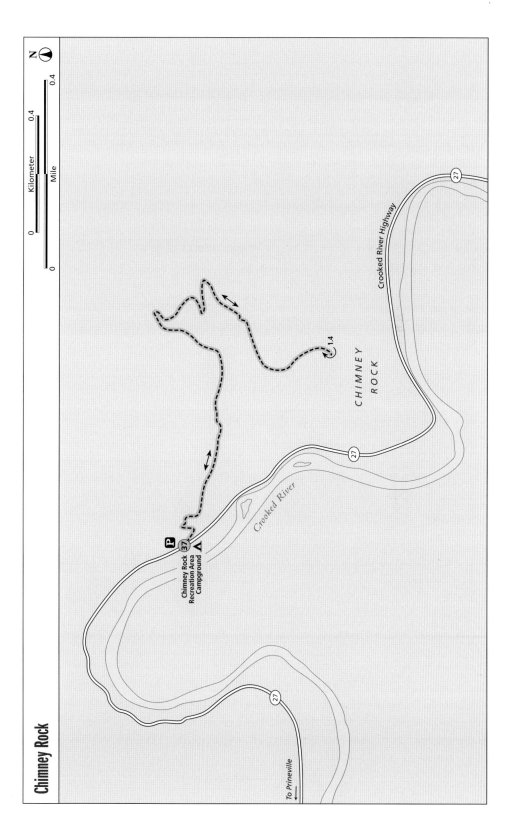

N

0   Kilometer   0.4

0   Mile   0.4

To Prineville

Crooked River

Chimney Rock
Recreation Area
Campground

P

37

CHIMNEY
ROCK

Crooked River Highway

27

27

27

1.4

You will enjoy nice views of the Crooked River canyon from the base of Chimney Rock.

Hike Information

Local Information: Prineville Chamber of Commerce, 185 NE 10th St., Prineville; (541) 447-6304

Restaurants: Crooked Roots Brewing, 420 N. Main St., Prineville; (541) 362-5583; crbrewing.com

38 Steins Pillar

This route takes you through a towering ponderosa pine forest to the base of Steins Pillar—a dramatic rock tower that is a definitive landmark in this area. The route also offers glimpses of the Central Cascade Mountains and the surrounding Ochoco Mountains. This hike offers solitude and scenery and is a great escape in an uncrowded part of the Central Oregon outdoors.

Start: Steins Pillar Trailhead off FR 500
Distance: 4.2-mile out-and-back
Hiking time: 2 to 3 hours
Difficulty: Moderate due to length of trail and moderate elevation gain
Trail surface: Dirt path
Best season: Year-round; snow may be present during the winter months
Other trail users: None

Canine compatibility: Leashed dogs permitted
Land status: Ochoco National Forest
Nearest town: Prineville
Fees and permits: None
Schedule: Open all hours
Maps: USGS Salt Butte and Steins Pillar
Trail contact: Ochoco National Forest, 3160 NE Third St., Prineville; (541) 416-6500; www.fs.usda.gov/ochoco

Finding the trailhead: From Main Street in Prineville, travel 9.4 miles east on US 26. Turn left (north) onto Mill Creek Road (FR 33). Travel 6.7 miles on Mill Creek Road (the road becomes gravel after 5.2 miles) to the junction with FR 500 (this road is easy to miss). Turn right onto FR 500 and continue 2.1 miles to the trailhead on the left side of the road. GPS: N44 23.699' / W120 37.416'

The Hike

Steins Pillar is a fascinating rock formation located in the heart of the Ochoco National Forest in the Ochoco Mountains. The 350-foot pillar is an important geologic remnant of the area's rich volcanic history. It is thought that this pillar was named after Major Enoch Steen of the US Army. In 1860 he was in charge of a raid against the Snake Indians, and he camped in Mill Creek Valley not far from Steins Pillar.

This route takes you through a scenic ponderosa pine forest to the base of Steins Pillar. The trail starts out fairly flat through a dry open forest of ponderosa pine. It slowly climbs and then begins descending, taking you past many rocky outcroppings. At 1.2 miles you'll pass a signed junction with a side trail that goes about 50 feet to a viewpoint. After 2.1 miles you will reach the base of Steins Pillar, which rises prominently above Mill Creek Valley. At the pillar's base look up to see why rock climbers find it such a tempting challenge. (The pillar was first climbed in 1950.) Admire the towering rock spire and then return on the same route.

Steins Pillar.

Miles and Directions

0.0 Start hiking on the dirt path next to the Steins Pillar trail sign.

1.2 Turn left at the signed viewpoint. Go about 50 feet and admire the mountain views, then return to the main trail and turn left to continue.

2.1 Arrive at the base of 350-foot Steins Pillar and your turnaround point. Retrace the same route back to the trailhead.

4.2 Arrive back at the trailhead.

Hike Information

Local Information: Prineville-Crook County Chamber of Commerce, 102 NW Second St., Prineville; (541) 447-6304; visitprineville.org

Restaurants: Solstice Brewing Company, 234 N. Main St., Prineville; (541) 233-0883; solsticebrewing.com

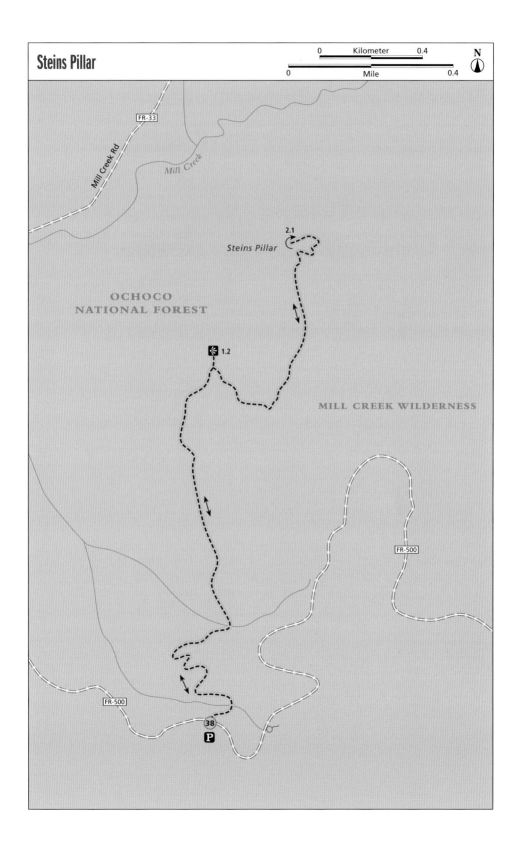

Steins Pillar

FR-33

Mill Creek Rd

Mill Creek

OCHOCO
NATIONAL FOREST

Steins Pillar

2.1

1.2

MILL CREEK WILDERNESS

FR-500

FR-500

38

0   Kilometer   0.4

0   Mile   0.4

N

39 Twin Pillars—Mill Creek Wilderness

The first 3 miles of this hike, a beautiful and peaceful walk through the Mill Creek Wilderness, includes wildlife, wildflowers, and a meandering stream. The remaining portion of the trail traverses a ponderosa pine forest interspersed with grassy meadows before arriving at the base of Twin Pillars, the eroded remnant of a volcano that erupted 40 to 50 million years ago.

Start: Twin Pillars Trail 380 trailhead near Wildcat Campground
Distance: 10.6-mile out-and-back
Hiking time: 4.5 to 6 hours
Difficulty: Difficult due to length of trail, multiple stream crossings, and the climb to the base of Twin Pillars
Trail surface: Dirt path with multiple stream crossings
Best season: June through Oct

Other trail users: Horseback riders
Canine compatibility: Leashed dogs permitted
Land status: Mill Creek Wilderness
Nearest town: Prineville
Fees and permits: None
Schedule: Open all hours
Maps: USGS Painted Hills
Trail contact: Ochoco National Forest, 3160 NE Third St., Prineville; (541) 416-6500; www.fs.usda.gov/ochoco

Finding the trailhead: From Prineville drive 9.1 miles east on US 26 to Mill Creek Road (FR 33). Turn left (north) and travel 10.6 miles to a fork in the road. Turn right at the sign for Wildcat Campground. Drive 0.1 mile and turn right into a gravel parking area at the trailhead. Wildcat Campground is another 0.3 mile past the parking area. GPS: N44 26.469' / W120 34.568'

The Hike

Located in the 17,000-acre Mill Creek Wilderness of Ochoco National Forest, the Twin Pillars Trail is a 10.6-mile out-and-back path along bubbling Mill Creek. The route passes through a forest of ponderosa pine, grand fir, and Douglas fir and up a steep ridge to the base of Twin Pillars—the double-spiked rock formation that constitutes the trail's namesake.

The trail begins with a series of creek crossings, so be sure to bring an old pair of tennis shoes or sandals to wear in the water. As you walk along the creek, you'll hear the cries of kingfishers protesting your presence on their home turf. Other birds in the area include pileated woodpeckers, wild turkeys, and northern goshawks. Pileated woodpeckers are the largest species of woodpecker and can be identified by their prominent red crests, black feathers, and white undersides. Northern goshawks, which weigh between 6 and 8 pounds and live up to 10 years, have slate-gray feathers and bright orange-red eyes outlined in white. You'll most

The book author hikes the Twin Pillars Trail with her 2 canine pals.

likely see them weaving in and out of the woodlands with great speed and finesse as they hunt for small birds and mammals. If you don't first see a northern goshawk, you may hear its distinctive "ca-ca-ca" hunting cry. Other wildlife in this pristine wilderness area include Rocky Mountain elk, mule deer, bobcats, cougars, and black bears.

As you continue on the trail, you'll pass green meadows of daisies, delicate purple aster, crimson penstemon, and bright purple thistle. Tall stalks of woolly mullein

Ken Skeen hikes the Twin Pillars Trail.

with their bright bunches of yellow flowers are also common. Shimmering green aspen trees grow in clusters along the banks of the creek, and cutthroat trout hang out in shady rock pools.

Three miles from the trailhead, the path turns away from Mill Creek and climbs steeply in a series of long and winding switchbacks for 2 miles up a ridge to the base of the 200-foot-tall Twin Pillars rock formation. Towering stands of Douglas fir and ponderosa pine grace the slopes of this ridge; below, wildflowers sprinkle open meadows with splashes of color.

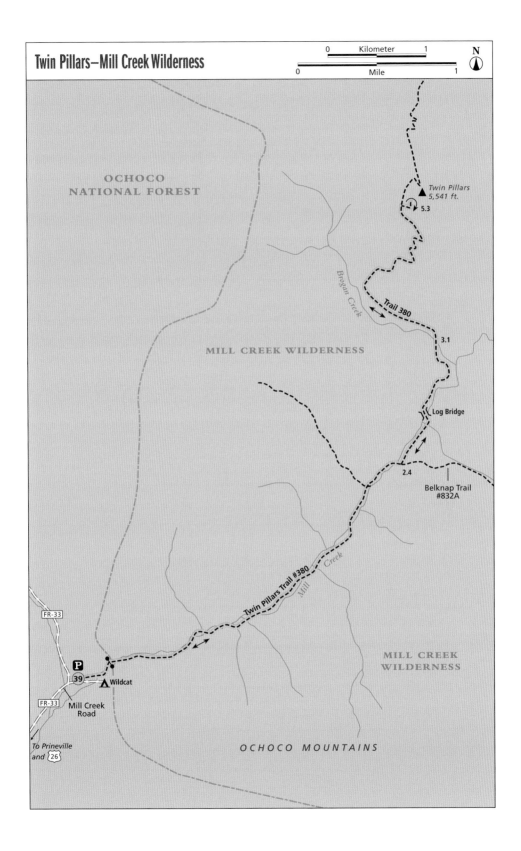

Twin Pillars–Mill Creek Wilderness

0   Kilometer   1

0   Mile   1

N

OCHOCO
NATIONAL FOREST

MILL CREEK WILDERNESS

Brogan Creek

Twin Pillars
5,541 ft.

5.3

Trail 380

3.1

Log Bridge

2.4

Belknap Trail
#832A

Twin Pillars Trail #380

Mill Creek

MILL CREEK
WILDERNESS

FR-33

P
39
Wildcat

FR-33

Mill Creek
Road

To Prineville
and 26

OCHOCO MOUNTAINS

Because of the length of this hike, you may want to complete the trail as an overnight backpack. There are many potential camping spots overlooking Mill Creek. Once you set up camp, you can wade in the creek, fish for trout, or just relax. The following day a light daypack is all you'll need for the remaining climb to the pillars' base. If you don't want to backpack, complete the trail in a day then pitch your tent at Wildcat Campground. The camping area is located just 0.3 mile northeast of the trailhead.

Miles and Directions

0.0   Start hiking on the signed Twin Pillars Trail 380.
0.1   Cross Mill Creek Road (FR 33) and continue straight.
0.2   Proceed through a green metal gate and enter the Mill Creek Wilderness.
0.3   Wade across Mill Creek. After the creek crossing the trail forks. Turn left.
0.8   Cross the creek.
0.9   Cross the creek.
1.1   Navigate another stream crossing.
1.2   Cross the creek. Proceed approximately 100 yards and cross again.
1.5   Cross the creek.
2.1   The trail forks. Turn left and continue along the main trail.
2.2   Arrive at another stream crossing. Logs are in place to help you cross. Walk another 50 yards and cross the stream again.
2.4   Cross the creek and arrive at a trail junction. Continue straight (left). (**Note:** Belknap Trail 832A goes right.)
2.5   Pass a sign on the left that reads "Twin Pillars 2 Miles."
2.7   Cross the creek on a log bridge.
2.9   The trail climbs steeply then veers away from the creek.
3.1   Cross Brogan Creek.
3.4   Enjoy a view of the Twin Pillars rock formation.
3.6   Cross a side creek.
4.0   Cross a very small side creek.
5.1   Turn right at the trail junction and scramble up a steep, rock-strewn slope to the base of the pillars.
5.3   Arrive at the base of Twin Pillars and your turnaround point. Enjoy a scenic view of the surrounding Ochoco Mountains, then retrace the same route back to the trailhead.
10.6 Arrive back at the trailhead.

Hike Information

Local Information: Prineville Chamber of Commerce, 185 NE 10th St, Prineville; (541) 447-6304
Restaurants: Crooked Roots Brewing, 420 N. Main St., Prineville; (541) 362-5583; crbrewing.com

40 Painted Hills Unit–John Day Fossil Beds

This route takes you on a 1.5-mile round-trip trek to the top of Carroll Rim, where you'll have a sweeping view of the painted hills and surrounding high desert country. There are many other short trails available in this area if you want to do additional exploring.

Start: Carroll Rim Trailhead off Bear Creek Road
Distance: 1.5-mile out-and-back
Hiking time: About 1 hour
Difficulty: Moderate due to elevation gain
Trail surface: Dirt path
Best season: Year-round
Other trail users: None
Canine compatibility: Leashed dogs permitted

Land status: National monument
Nearest town: Mitchell
Fees and permits: None
Schedule: Open all hours
Maps: USGS Painted Hills
Trail contact: John Day Fossil Beds National Monument, 32651 Hwy. 19, Kimberly; (541) 987-2333; www.nps.gov/joda/planyourvisit/index.htm

Finding the trailhead: From Prineville travel 45.2 miles east on US 26 to the junction with Burnt Ranch Road where a sign indicates "John Day Fossil Beds National Monument–Painted Hills Unit." Turn left (north) and go 5.7 miles. Turn left onto Bear Creek Road and proceed 0.9 mile to the turnoff for the Carroll Rim Trailhead. Turn left and then take an immediate right into the gravel parking area on the right. The Carroll Rim Trail begins on the opposite side of the road from the parking area. The 0.5-mile out-and-back Painted Hills Overlook Trail can also be accessed from this parking area. Follow the road signs to reach the Painted Cove Trail, Leaf Hill Trail, and Red Hill Trail. GPS: N44 39.25' / W120 15.11'

The Hike

This hike takes you to the summit of Carroll Rim, a high ridge consisting of John Day ignimbrite, better known as welded tuff. More than 28 million years ago, a volcano to the west erupted and hurled hot ash, debris, and gases into the air, which then landed and cooled to form a glass-like layer.

One of the most striking features in the Painted Hills Unit is the round, multicolored hills of colorful claystone. Over millions of years, after the volcanoes deposited the layers of ash, the forces of nature carved and shaped the hills that you see today. Elements such as aluminum, silicon, iron, magnesium, manganese, sodium, calcium, and titanium have combined to produce minerals that have unique properties and colors.

The colorful painted hills are one of the many highlights in the Painted Hills Unit.

Follow the signed trail for 0.75 mile to the top of the rim. From the top you'll be able to see Sutton Mountain, which rises prominently to the east. Return on the same route back to the trailhead.

Miles and Directions

0.0   Start hiking on the Carroll Rim Trail, which is accessed across the road from the parking area.

0.75   Reach the summit and turnaround point of the Carroll Rim Trail. After enjoying the views, head back on the same trail.

1.5   Arrive back at the trailhead.

Options

If you feel like exploring more trails, there are many options available. You can take a short jaunt on the 0.5-mile out-and-back Painted Hills Overlook Trail, which

Ken Skeen with Bear and Tiz on the Painted Hills Overlook Trail.

takes you up a gentle ridge and along the way includes several viewpoints of the stunning multicolored hills. If you want a close-up view of one of these unique painted hills, take a walk on the 0.25-mile Painted Cove Trail loop. A brochure and corresponding trail markers offer an in-depth look at these geologic formations. For instance, the colors of the hills change with the weather. When it rains, the clay absorbs water, causing more light reflection and changing the color of the hills from red to pink and from light brown to yellow-gold. As the hills dry out, the soil contracts, causing surface cracking that diffuses the light and deepens the color of the hills. The purple layer in the hill is the weathered remains of a rhyolite lava flow. Other colored bands in the hillside are due to differences in mineral content and weathering. Plants can't grow on the painted hills because the clay is so dense that moisture can't penetrate the surface and also because the clay soil is nutrition-ally poor.

For fossils check out the 0.25-mile-long Leaf Hill Trail and its collection of ancient plants. The trail circles a small hill of loose shale deposits. While at first the

The Painted Hills Overlook Trail offers some of the best viewpoints of the Painted Hills.

hill seems somewhat unremarkable, a closer look reveals secrets to the plants that once dominated here. The shales present in this hill were formed about 33 million years ago from lake-deposited volcanic ash. Thirty-five species of fossilized plants can be found at Leaf Hill, with alder, beech, maple, and the extinct hornbeam most prevalent. Other specimens include elm, rose, oak, grape, fern, redwood, and pine. Scientists have analyzed these plant fossils and concluded that this group of plants closely resembles two types of modern forests found in China—the mixed northern hardwood forest and the mixed mesophytic forest. Comparing the mix of plant species to these two modern forests indicates that this area had a much higher rainfall (up to 40 inches), milder temperatures, and a warmer climate than that found here today. (Today the area receives about 12 to 15 inches of rain a year and experiences more extreme temperature variations.) In addition, the vegetation that grows here today is made up of high desert–type plants—juniper, sagebrush, and grasses.

The 0.4-mile Red Hill Trail gives you another interesting perspective of the striking red clay that makes up this unique landscape.

Hike Information

Local Information: Prineville Chamber of Commerce, 185 NE 10th St., Prineville; (541) 447-6304

Restaurants: Crooked Roots Brewing, 420 N. Main St., Prineville; (541) 362-5583; crbrewing.com

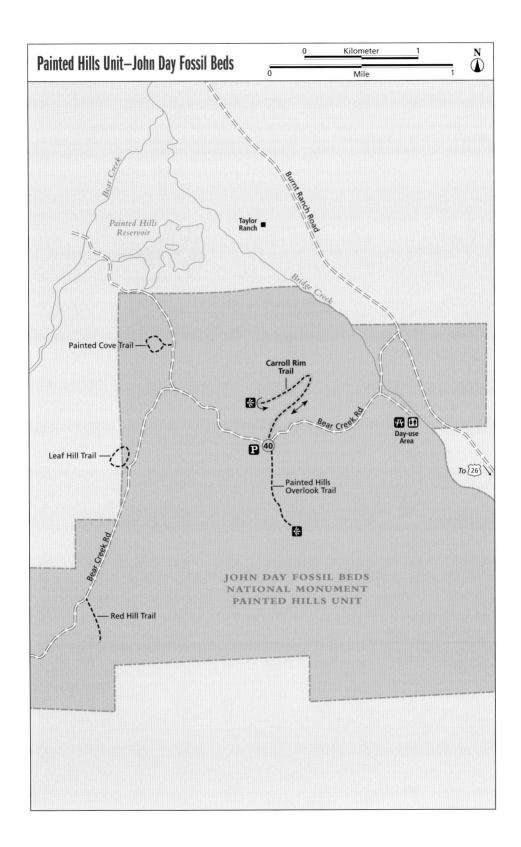

Painted Hills Unit–John Day Fossil Beds

Bear Creek

Painted Hills Reservoir

Taylor Ranch

Burnt Ranch Road

Bridge Creek

Painted Cove Trail

Carroll Rim Trail

Bear Creek Rd

Day-use Area

To 26

Leaf Hill Trail

P 40

Painted Hills Overlook Trail

Bear Creek Rd

Red Hill Trail

JOHN DAY FOSSIL BEDS
NATIONAL MONUMENT
PAINTED HILLS UNIT

The Art of Hiking

The following section will help you understand better what it means to "do what you can" while still making the most of your hiking experience. Anyone can take a hike, but hiking safely and well is an art requiring preparation and proper equipment.

Trail Etiquette

Zero impact. Always leave an area just like you found it—if not better than you found it. Avoid camping in fragile, alpine meadows and along the banks of streams and lakes. Use a camp stove rather than building a wood fire. Pack up all of your trash and extra food. Bury human waste at least 100 feet from water sources under 6 to 8 inches of topsoil. Don't bathe with soap in a lake or stream—use prepackaged moistened towels to wipe off sweat and dirt, or bathe in the water without soap.

Stay on the trail. It's true, a path anywhere leads nowhere new, but purists will just have to get over it. Paths serve an important purpose; they limit impact on natural areas. Straying from a designated trail may seem innocent, but it can cause damage to sensitive areas—damage that may take years to recover, if it can recover at all. Even simple shortcuts can be destructive. So, please, stay on the trail.

Leave no weeds. Noxious weeds tend to overtake other plants, which in turn affects animals and birds that depend on them for food. To minimize the spread of noxious weeds, hikers should regularly clean their boots, tents, packs, and hiking poles of mud and seeds. Also brush your dog to remove any weed seeds before heading off into a new area.

Keep your dog under control. Always obey leash laws and be sure to bury your dog's waste or pack it in resealable plastic bags.

Respect other trail users. Often you're not the only one on the trail. With the rise in popularity of multiuse trails, you'll have to learn a new kind of respect, beyond the nod and "hello" approach you may be used to. First investigate whether you're on a multiuse trail, and assume the appropriate precautions. When you encounter motorized vehicles (ATVs, motorcycles, and 4WDs), be alert. Though they should always yield to the hiker, often they're going too fast or are too lost in the buzz of their engine to react to your presence. If you hear activity ahead, step off the trail, just to be safe. Note that you're not likely to hear a mountain biker coming, so be prepared and know ahead of time whether you share the trail with them. Cyclists should always yield to hikers, but that's little comfort to the hiker. Be aware. When you approach horses or pack animals on the trail, always step quietly off the trail, preferably on the downhill side, and let them pass. If you're wearing a large backpack, it's often a good idea to sit down. To some animals, a hiker wearing a large backpack might appear threatening. Many national forests allow domesticated grazing, usually for sheep and cattle. Make sure your dog doesn't harass these animals, and respect ranchers' rights while you're enjoying yours.

Getting into Shape

Unless you want to be sore—and possibly have to shorten your trip or vacation—be sure to get into shape before a big hike. If you're terribly out of shape, start a walking program early, preferably 8 weeks in advance. Start with a 15-minute walk during your lunch hour or after work and gradually increase your walking time to an hour. You should also increase your elevation gain. Walking briskly up hills really strengthens your leg muscles and gets your heart rate up. If you work in a multistory office building, take the stairs instead of the elevator. If you prefer going to a gym, walk the treadmill or use a stair machine. You can further increase your strength and endurance by walking with a loaded backpack. Stationary exercises you might consider are squats, leg lifts, sit-ups, and push-ups. Other good ways to get in shape include biking, running, aerobics, and, of course, short hikes. Stretching before and after a hike keeps muscles flexible and helps avoid injuries.

Preparedness

It's been said that failing to plan means planning to fail. So do take the necessary time to plan your trip. Whether going on a short day hike or an extended backpack trip, always prepare for the worst.

Water. Even in frigid conditions, you need at least 2 quarts of water a day to function efficiently. Add heat and taxing terrain and you can bump that figure up to 1 gallon. That's simply a base to work from—your metabolism and your level of conditioning can raise or lower that amount. Unless you know your level, assume that you need 1 gallon of water a day.

Now, where do you plan on getting the water? Preferably not from natural water sources. These sources can be loaded with intestinal disturbers, such as bacteria, viruses, and fertilizers. *Giardia lamblia,* the most common of these disturbers, is a protozoan parasite that lives part of its life cycle as a cyst in water sources. The parasite spreads when mammals defecate in water sources. Once ingested, giardia can induce cramping, diarrhea, vomiting, and fatigue within 2 days to 2 weeks after ingestion. Giardiasis is treatable with prescription drugs. If you believe you've contracted giardiasis, see a doctor immediately.

Treating water. The best and easiest solution to avoid polluted water is to carry your water with you. Yet, depending on the nature of your hike and the duration, this may not be an option—1 gallon of water weighs 8 ½ pounds. In that case, you'll need to look into treating water. Regardless of which method you choose, you should always carry some water with you in case of an emergency. Save this reserve until you absolutely need it.

There are three methods of treating water: boiling, chemical treatment, and filtering. If you boil water, it's recommended that you do so for 10 to 15 minutes. This is often impractical because you're forced to exhaust a great deal of your fuel supply. You can opt for chemical treatment, which will kill giardia but will not take care of other chemical pollutants. Another drawback to chemical treatments is the unpleasant taste of the water after it's treated. You can remedy this by adding powdered drink mix to the water. Filters are the preferred method for treating water. Many filters remove giardia, organic and inorganic contaminants, and don't leave an aftertaste. Water filters are far from perfect as they can easily become clogged or leak if a gasket wears out. It's always a good idea to carry a backup supply of chemical treatment tablets in case your filter decides to quit on you.

Food. If we're talking about survival, you can go days without food, as long as you have water. But we're also talking about comfort. Try to avoid foods that are high in sugar and fat like candy bars and potato chips. These food types are harder to digest and are low in nutritional value. Instead, bring along foods that are easy to pack, nutritious, and high in energy (e.g., bagels, nutrition bars, dehydrated fruit, gorp, and jerky). If you are on an overnight trip, easy-to-fix dinners include rice mixes with dehydrated potatoes, corn, pasta with cheese sauce, and soup mixes. For a tasty breakfast, you can fix hot oatmeal with brown sugar and reconstituted milk powder topped off with banana chips. If you like a hot drink in the morning, bring along herbal tea bags or hot chocolate. If you are a coffee junkie, you can purchase coffee that is packaged like tea bags or in a powder form. You can prepackage all of your meals in heavy-duty resealable plastic bags to keep food from spilling in your pack. These bags can be reused to pack out trash.

Shelter. The type of shelter you choose depends less on the conditions than on your tolerance for discomfort. Shelter comes in many forms—tent, tarp, lean-to, bivy sack, cabin, cave, etc. If you're camping in the desert, a bivy sack may suffice, but if you're above the treeline and a storm is approaching, a better choice is a three- or four-season tent. Tents are the logical and most popular choice for most backpackers as they're lightweight and packable—and you can rest assured that you always have shelter from the elements. Before you leave on your trip, anticipate what the weather and terrain will be like and plan for the type of shelter that will work best for your comfort level (see "Equipment" later in this section).

Finding a campsite. If there are established campsites, stick to those. If not, start looking for a campsite early—around 3:30 or 4 p.m. Stop at the first decent site you see. Depending on the area, it could be a long time before you find another suitable location. Pitch your camp in an area that's level. Make sure the area is at least 200 feet from fragile areas like lakeshores, meadows, and stream banks. And try to avoid areas thick in underbrush, as they can harbor insects and provide cover for approaching animals.

If you are camping in stormy, rainy weather, look for a rock outcrop or a shelter in the trees to keep the wind from blowing your tent all night. Be sure that you don't camp under trees with dead limbs that might break off on top of you. Also, try to find an area that has an absorbent surface, such as sandy soil or forest duff. This, in addition to camping on a surface with a slight angle, will provide better drainage. By all means, don't dig trenches to provide drainage around your tent—remember, you're practicing zero-impact camping.

If you're in bear country, steer clear of creek beds or animal paths. If you see any signs of a bear's presence (i.e., scat, footprints), relocate. You'll need to find a campsite near a tall tree where you can hang your food and other items that may attract bears such as deodorant, toothpaste, or soap. Carry a lightweight nylon rope with which to hang your food. As a rule, you should hang your food at least 20 feet from the ground and 5 feet away from the tree trunk. You can put food and other items in a waterproof stuff sack and tie one end of the rope to the stuff sack. To get the other end of the rope over the tree branch, tie a good-size rock to it, and gently toss the rock over the tree branch. Pull the stuff sack up until it reaches the top of the branch and tie it off securely. Don't hang your food near your tent! If possible, hang your food at least 100 feet away from your campsite. Alternatives to hanging your food are bear-proof plastic tubes and metal bear boxes.

Last, think of comfort. Lie down on the ground where you intend to sleep and see if it's a good fit. For morning warmth (and a nice view to wake up to), have your tent face east.

First Aid

- ☐ adhesive bandages
- ☐ moleskin or duct tape
- ☐ various sterile gauze and dressings
- ☐ white surgical tape
- ☐ an Ace bandage
- ☐ antihistamine
- ☐ aspirin
- ☐ Betadine solution
- ☐ a first-aid manual
- ☐ antacid tablets

- ☐ tweezers
- ☐ scissors
- ☐ antibacterial wipes
- ☐ triple antibiotic ointment
- ☐ plastic gloves
- ☐ sterile cotton-tip applicators
- ☐ syrup of ipecac (to induce vomiting)
- ☐ thermometer
- ☐ wire splint

Here are a few tips for dealing with and hopefully preventing certain ailments.

Sunburn. Take along sunscreen or sunblock, protective clothing, and a wide-brimmed hat. If you do get a sunburn, treat the area with aloe vera gel, and protect the area from further sun exposure. At higher elevations the sun's radiation can be particularly damaging to skin. Remember that your eyes are vulnerable to this radiation as well. Sunglasses can be a good way to prevent headaches and permanent eye damage from the sun, especially in places where light-colored rock or patches of snow reflect light up in your face.

Blisters. Be prepared to take care of these hike spoilers by carrying moleskin (a lightly padded adhesive), gauze and tape, or adhesive bandages. An effective way to apply moleskin is to cut out a circle of moleskin and remove the center—like a doughnut—and place it over the blistered area. Cutting the center out will reduce the pressure applied to the sensitive skin. Other products can help you combat blisters. Some are applied to suspicious hot spots before a blister forms to help decrease friction to that area, while others are applied to the blister after it has popped to help prevent further irritation.

Insect bites and stings. You can treat most insect bites and stings by applying hydrocortisone 1 percent cream topically and taking a pain medication such as ibuprofen or acetaminophen to reduce swelling. If you forgot to pack these items, a cold compress or a paste of mud and ashes can sometimes assuage the itching and discomfort. Remove any stingers by using tweezers or scraping the area with your fingernail or a knife blade. Don't pinch the area as you'll only spread the venom.

Some hikers are highly sensitive to bites and stings and may have a serious allergic reaction that can be life threatening. Symptoms of a serious allergic reaction can include wheezing, an asthmatic attack, and shock. The treatment for this severe type of reaction is epinephrine. If you know that you are sensitive to bites and stings, carry a prepackaged kit of epinephrine, which can be obtained only by prescription from your doctor.

Ticks. Ticks can carry diseases such as Rocky Mountain spotted fever and Lyme disease. The best defense is, of course, prevention. If you know you're going to be hiking through an area littered with ticks, wear long pants and a long-sleeved shirt. You can apply a permethrin repellent to your clothing and a deet repellent to exposed skin. There are also many natural alternatives for insect protection that do not have deet as an ingredient. These natural repellents work very well—just keep in mind that they need to be reapplied every few hours. At the end of your hike, do a spot-check for ticks (and insects in general). If you do find a tick, coat the insect with petroleum jelly or tree sap to cut off its air supply. The tick should release its hold, but if it doesn't, grab the head of the tick firmly—with a pair of tweezers if you have them—and gently pull it away from the skin with a twisting motion. Sometimes the mouth parts linger, embedded in your skin. If this happens, try to remove them with a disinfected needle. Clean the affected area with an antibacterial cleanser and then apply triple antibiotic ointment. Monitor the area for a few days. If irritation persists or a white spot develops, see a doctor for possible infection.

Poison ivy, oak, and sumac. These skin irritants can be found most anywhere in North America and come in the form of a bush or a vine, having leaflets in groups of three, five, seven, or nine. Learn how to spot the plants. The oil they secrete can cause an allergic reaction in the form of blisters, usually about 12 hours after exposure. The itchy rash can last from 10 days to several weeks. The best defense against these irritants is to wear clothing that covers the arms, legs, and torso. For summer, zip-off cargo pants come in handy. There are also nonprescription lotions you can apply to exposed skin that guard against the effects of poison ivy/oak/sumac and can be washed off with soap and water. If you think you were in contact with the plants, after hiking (or even on the trail during longer hikes) wash with soap and water. Taking a hot shower with soap after you return home from your hike will also help remove any lingering oil from your skin. Should you contract a rash from any of these plants, use an antihistamine to reduce the itching. If the rash is localized, create a light bleach/water wash to dry up the area. If the rash has spread, either tough it out or see your doctor about getting a dose of cortisone (available both orally and by injection).

Snakebites. Snakebites are rare in North America. Unless startled or provoked, the majority of snakes will not bite. If you are wise to their habitats and keep a careful eye on the trail, you should be just fine. When stepping over logs, first step on the log, making sure you can see what's on the other side before stepping down. Though your chances of being struck are slim, it's wise to know what to do in the event you are.

If a nonvenomous snake bites you, allow the wound to bleed a small amount and then cleanse the wounded area with a Betadine solution (10 percent povidone iodine). Rinse the wound with clean water (preferably) or fresh urine (it might sound ugly, but it's sterile). Once the area is clean, cover it with triple antibiotic ointment and a clean bandage. Remember, most residual damage from snakebites, venomous or otherwise, comes from infection, not the snake's venom. Keep the area as clean as possible and get medical attention immediately.

If you are bitten by a venomous snake, remove the toxin with a suctioning device, found in a snakebite kit. If you do not have such a device, squeeze the wound—do *not* use your mouth for suction, as the venom will enter your bloodstream through the vessels under the tongue and head straight for your heart. Then, clean the wound just as you would a nonvenomous bite. Tie a clean band of cloth snugly around the afflicted appendage, about an inch or so above the bite (or the rim of the swelling). This is *not* a tourniquet—you want to simply slow the blood flow, not cut it off. Loosen the band if numbness ensues. Remove the band for a minute and reapply a little higher every 10 minutes.

If it is your friend who's been bitten, treat him or her for shock—make the person comfortable, have him or her lie down, elevate the legs, and keep him or her warm. Avoid applying anything cold to the bite wound. Immobilize the affected area and remove any constricting items such as rings, watches, or restrictive clothing—swelling may occur. Once your friend is stable and relatively calm, hike out to get help. The victim should get treatment within 12 hours, ideally, which usually consists of a tetanus shot, antivenin, and antibiotics.

If you are alone and struck by a venomus snake, stay calm. Hysteria will only quicken the venom's spread. Follow the procedure above, and do your best to reach help. When hiking out, don't run—you'll only increase the flow of blood throughout your system. Instead, walk calmly.

Dehydration. Have you ever hiked in hot weather and had a roaring headache and felt fatigued after only a few miles? More than likely you were dehydrated. Symptoms of dehydration include fatigue, headache, and decreased coordination and judgment. When you are hiking, your body's rate of fluid loss depends on the outside temperature, humidity, altitude, and your activity level. On average, a hiker walking in warm weather will lose 4 liters of fluid a day. That fluid loss is easily replaced by normal consumption of liquids and food. However, if a hiker is walking briskly in hot, dry weather and hauling a heavy pack, he or she can lose 1 to 3 liters of water an hour. It's important to always carry plenty of water and to stop often and drink fluids regularly, even if you aren't thirsty.

Heat exhaustion. The result of a loss of large amounts of electrolytes, heat exhaustion often occurs if a hiker is dehydrated and has been under heavy exertion. Common symptoms of heat exhaustion include cramping, exhaustion, fatigue, lightheadedness, and nausea. You can treat heat exhaustion by getting out of the sun and drinking an electrolyte solution made up of one teaspoon of salt and one tablespoon of sugar dissolved in a liter of water. Drink this solution slowly over a period of 1 hour. Drinking plenty of fluids (preferably an electrolyte solution/sports drink) can prevent heat exhaustion. Avoid hiking during the hottest parts of the day, and wear breathable clothing, a wide-brimmed hat, and sunglasses.

Hypothermia. One of the biggest dangers in the backcountry is hypothermia, especially for day hikers in the summertime. That may sound strange, but imagine starting out on a hike in midsummer when it's sunny and 80 degrees out. You're clad in nylon shorts and a cotton T-shirt. About halfway through your hike, the sky begins to cloud up, and in the next hour a light drizzle begins to fall and the wind starts to pick up. Before you know it, you are soaking wet and shivering—the perfect recipe for hypothermia. More advanced signs include decreased coordination, slurred speech, and blurred vision. When a victim's temperature falls below 92 degrees, the blood pressure and pulse plummet, possibly leading to coma and death.

To avoid hypothermia, always bring a windproof/rainproof shell, a fleece jacket, tights made of a breathable, synthetic fiber, gloves, and hat when you are hiking in the mountains. Learn to adjust your clothing layers based on the temperature. If you are climbing uphill at a moderate pace, you will stay warm, but when you stop for a break you'll become cold quickly, unless you add more layers of clothing.

If a hiker is showing advanced signs of hypothermia, dress him or her in dry clothes and make sure he or she is wearing a hat and gloves. Place the person in a sleeping bag in a tent or shelter that will protect him or her from the wind and other elements. Give the person warm fluids to drink and keep him awake.

Frostbite. When the mercury dips below 32 degrees F, your extremities begin to chill. If a persistent chill attacks a localized area, say, your hands or your toes, the circulatory system reacts by cutting off blood flow to the affected area—the idea being to protect and preserve the body's overall temperature. And so it's death by attrition for the affected area. Ice crystals start to form from the water in the cells of the neglected tissue. Deprived of heat, nourishment, and now water, the tissue literally starves. This is frostbite.

Prevention is your best defense against this situation. Most prone to frostbite are your face, hands, and feet, so protect these areas well. Wool is the material of choice because it provides ample air space for insulation and draws moisture away from the skin. Synthetic fabrics, however, have recently made great strides in the cold weather clothing market. Do your research. A pair of light silk liners under your regular gloves is a good trick for keeping warm. They afford some additional warmth, but more importantly, they'll allow you to remove your mitts for tedious work without exposing the skin.

If your feet or hands start to feel cold or numb due to the elements, warm them as quickly as possible. Place cold hands under your armpits or bury them in your crotch. If your feet are cold, change your socks. If there's plenty of room in your boots, add another pair of socks. Do remember, though, that constricting your feet in tight boots can restrict blood flow and actually make your feet colder more quickly. Your socks need to have breathing room if they're going to be effective. Dead air provides insulation. If your face is cold, place your warm hands over your face, or simply wear a head stocking.

Should your skin go numb and start to appear white and waxy, chances are you've got or are developing frostbite. Don't try to thaw the area unless you can maintain the warmth. In other words, don't stop to warm up your frostbitten feet only to head back on the trail. You'll do more damage than good. Tests have shown that hikers who walked on thawed feet did more harm, and endured more pain, than hikers who left the affected areas alone. Do your best to get out of the cold entirely and seek medical attention—which usually consists of performing a rapid rewarming in water for 20 to 30 minutes.

The overall objective in preventing both hypothermia and frostbite is to keep the body's core warm. Protect key areas where heat escapes, like the top of the head, and maintain the proper nutrition level. Foods that are high in calories aid the body in producing heat. Never smoke or drink when you're in situations where the cold is threatening. By affecting blood flow, these activities ultimately cool the body's core temperature.

Altitude sickness (AMS). High, lofty peaks, clear alpine lakes, and vast mountain views beckon hikers to the high country. But those who like to venture high may become victims of altitude sickness (also known as acute mountain sickness—AMS). Altitude sickness is your body's reaction to insufficient oxygen in the blood due to decreased barometric pressure. While some hikers may feel lightheaded, nauseous, and experience shortness of breath at 7,000 feet, others may not experience these symptoms until they reach 10,000 feet or higher.

Slowing your ascent to high places and giving your body a chance to acclimatize to the higher elevations can prevent altitude sickness. For example, if you live at sea level and are planning a weeklong backpacking trip to elevations between 7,000 and 12,000 feet, start by staying below 7,000 feet for one night, then move to between 7,000 and 10,000 feet for another night or two. Avoid strenuous exertion and alcohol to give your body a chance to adjust to the new altitude. It's also important to eat light food and drink plenty of nonalcoholic fluids, preferably water. Loss of appetite at high altitudes is common, but you must eat!

Most hikers who experience mild to moderate AMS develop a headache and/ or nausea, grow lethargic, and have problems sleeping. The treatment for AMS is simple: Stop heading uphill. Keep eating and drinking water and take meds for the headache. You actually need to take more breaths at altitude than at sea level, so breathe a little faster, without hyperventilating. If symptoms don't improve over 24 to 48 hours, descend. Once a victim descends about 2,000 to 3,000 feet, his signs will usually begin to diminish.

Severe AMS comes in two forms: high-altitude pulmonary edema (HAPE) and high-altitude cerebral edema (HACE). HAPE, an accumulation of fluid in the lungs, can occur above 8,000 feet. Symptoms include rapid heart rate, shortness of breath at rest, AMS symptoms, dry cough developing into a wet cough, gurgling sounds, flulike or bronchitis symptoms, and lack of muscle coordination. HAPE is life threatening, so descend immediately, at least 2,000 to 4,000 feet. HACE usually occurs above 12,000 feet but sometimes occurs above 10,000 feet. Symptoms are similar to HAPE but also include seizures, hallucinations, paralysis, and vision disturbances. Descend immediately—HACE is also life threatening.

Hantavirus pulmonary syndrome (HPS). Deer mice spread the virus that causes HPS, and humans contract it from breathing it in, usually when they've disturbed an area with dust and mice feces from nests or surfaces with mice drop-pings or urine. Exposure to large numbers of rodents and their feces or urine presents the greatest risk. As hikers, we sometimes enter old buildings, and often deer mice live in these places. We may not be around long enough to be exposed, but do be aware of this disease. About half the people who develop HPS die. Symptoms are flulike and appear about 2 to 3 weeks after exposure. After initial symptoms a dry cough and shortness of breath follow. Breathing is difficult. If you even think you might have HPS, see a doctor immediately!

Natural Hazards

Besides tripping over a rock or tree root on the trail, there are some real haz-ards to be aware of while hiking. Even if where you're hiking doesn't have the plethora of venomous snakes and plants, insects, and grizzly bears found in other parts of the United States, there are a few weather conditions and predators you may need to take into account.

Lightning. Thunderstorms build over the mountains almost every day during the summer. Lightning is generated by thunderheads and can strike without warn-ing, even several miles away from the nearest overhead cloud. The best rule of thumb is to start leaving exposed peaks, ridges, and canyon rims by about noon. This time can vary a little depending on storm buildup. Keep an eye on cloud formation and don't underestimate how fast a storm can build. The bigger they get, the more likely a thunderstorm will happen. Lightning takes the path of least resistance, so if you're the high point, it might choose you. Ducking under a rock overhang is dangerous as you form the shortest path between the rock and ground. If you dash below treeline, avoid standing under the only or the tallest tree. If you are caught above treeline, stay away from anything metal you might be carrying. Move down off the ridge slightly to a low, treeless point and squat until the storm passes. If you have an insulating pad, squat on it. Avoid having both your hands and feet touching the ground at once and never lay flat. If you hear a buzzing sound or feel your hair standing on end, move quickly as an electrical charge is building up.

Flash floods. On July 31, 1976, a torrential downpour dumped tons of water into the Big Thompson watershed near Estes Park, Colorado. Within hours, a wall of water moved down the narrow canyon killing 139 people and causing more than $30 million in property damage. The spooky thing about flash floods, especially in western canyons, is that they can appear out of nowhere from a storm many miles away. While hiking or driving in canyons, keep an eye on the weather. Always climb to safety if danger threatens. Flash floods usually subside quickly, so be patient and don't cross a swollen stream.

Bears. Most of the United States (outside of the Pacific Northwest and parts of the Northern Rockies) does not have a grizzly bear population, although some rumors exist about sightings where there should be none. Black bears are plentiful, however. Here are some tips in case you and a bear scare each other. Most of all, avoid scaring a bear. Watch for bear tracks (five toes) and droppings (sizable with leaves, partly digested berries, seeds, and/or animal fur). Talk or sing where visibility or hearing are limited. Keep a clean camp, hang food, and don't sleep in the clothes you wore while cooking. Be especially careful in spring to avoid getting between a mother and her cubs. In late summer and fall, bears are busy eating berries and acorns to fatten up for winter, so be extra careful around berry bushes and oakbrush. If you do encounter a bear, move away slowly while facing the bear, talk softly, and avoid direct eye contact. Give the bear room to escape. Since bears are very curious, it might stand upright to get a better whiff of you, and it may even charge you to try to intimidate you. Try to stay calm. If a bear does attack you, fight back with anything you have handy. Unleashed dogs have been known to come running back to their owners with a bear close behind. Keep your dog on a leash or leave it at home.

Mountain lions. Usually elusive and quiet, lions rarely attack people. If you meet a lion, give it a chance to escape. Stay calm and talk firmly to it. Back away slowly while facing the lion. If you run, you'll only encourage the curious cat to chase you. Make yourself look large by opening a jacket, if you have one, or waving your hiking poles. If the lion behaves aggressively, throw stones, sticks, or whatever you can while remaining tall. If a lion does attack, fight for your life with anything you can grab.

Moose. Because moose have very few natural predators, they don't fear humans like other animals. You might find moose in sagebrush and wetter areas of willow, aspen, and pine, or in beaver habitats. Mothers with calves, as well as bulls during mating season, can be particularly aggressive. If a moose threatens you, back away slowly and talk calmly to it. Keep your pets away from moose.

Other considerations. Hunting is a popular sport in the United States, especially during rifle season in October and November. Hiking is still enjoyable in those months in many areas, so just take a few precautions. First, learn when the different hunting seasons start and end in the area in which you'll be hiking. During this time frame, be sure to wear at least a blaze orange hat, and possibly put an orange vest over your pack. Don't be surprised to see hunters in camo outfits carrying bows or muzzle-loading rifles around during their season. If you would feel more comfortable without hunters around, hike in national parks and monuments or state and local parks where hunting is not allowed.

Navigation

Whether you are going on a short hike in a familiar area or planning a week-long backpack trip, you should always be equipped with the proper navigational equipment—at the very least a detailed map and a sturdy compass.

Maps. There are many different types of maps available to help you find your way on the trail. Easiest to find are Forest Service maps and BLM (Bureau of Land Management) maps. These maps tend to cover large areas, so be sure they are detailed enough for your particular trip. You can also obtain national park maps as well as high-quality maps from private companies and trail groups. These maps can be obtained either from outdoor stores or ranger stations.

U.S. Geological Survey topographic maps are particularly popular with hikers—especially serious backcountry hikers. These maps contain the standard map symbols such as roads, lakes, and rivers, as well as contour lines that show the details of the trail terrain like ridges, valleys, passes, and mountain peaks. The 7.5-minute series (1 inch on the map equals approximately 2/5 mile on the ground) provides the closest inspection available. USGS maps are available by mail (U.S. Geological Survey, Map Distribution Branch, P.O. Box 25286, Denver, CO 80225), or at store.usgs.gov.

If you want to check out the high-tech world of maps, you can purchase topographic maps from the web. These software-mapping programs let you select a route on your computer, print it out, then take it with you on the trail. Some software mapping programs let you insert symbols and labels, download waypoints from a GPS unit, and export the maps to other software programs. If you are interested in learning more about mapping programs, you may want to try Garmin BaseCamp (garmin.com/us/products/onthetrail/basecamp). Google Earth is a very popular navigation program that you can download from the web by visiting google.com/earth/index.html. There are also very good apps you can download to your smartphone such as Gaia GPS (www.gaiagps.com) and Backcountry Navigator (www.backcountrynavigator.com).

The art of map reading is a skill that you can develop by first practicing in an area you are familiar with. To begin, orient the map so the map is lined up in the correct direction (i.e., north on the map is lined up with true north). Next, familiarize yourself with the map symbols and try to match them up with terrain features around you such as a high ridge, mountain peak, river, or lake. If you are practicing with a USGS map, notice the contour lines. On gentler terrain these contour lines are spaced farther apart, and on steeper terrain they are closer together. Pick a short loop trail, and stop frequently to check your position on the map. As you practice map reading, you'll learn how to anticipate a steep section on the trail or a good place to take a rest break, and so on.

Compasses. First off, the sun is not a substitute for a compass. So, what kind of compass should you have? Here are some characteristics you should look for: a rectangular base with detailed scales, a liquid-filled housing, protective housing, a sighting line on the mirror, luminous alignment and back-bearing arrows, a luminous north-seeking arrow, and a well-defined bezel ring.

You can learn compass basics by reading the detailed instructions included with your compass. If you want to fine-tune your compass skills, sign up for an orienteering class or purchase a book on compass reading. Once you've learned the basic skills of using a compass, remember to practice these skills before you head into the backcountry.

If you are a klutz at using a compass, you may be interested in checking out the technical wizardry of the GPS (Global Positioning System) device or GPS watch. The GPS was developed by the Pentagon and works off twenty-four NAVSTAR satellites, which were designed to guide missiles to their targets. A GPS device is a handheld unit that calculates your latitude and longitude with the easy press of a button. The Department of Defense used to scramble the satellite signals a bit to prevent civilians (and spies!) from getting extremely accurate readings, but that practice was discontinued in May 2000, and GPS units now provide nearly pinpoint accuracy (within 30 to 60 feet).

In general, all GPS units have a display screen and keypad where you input information. In addition to acting as a compass, the unit allows you to plot your route, easily retrace your path, track your travel speed, find the mileage between waypoints, and calculate the total mileage of your route as well as elevation change. Some GPS devices have cameras so you can take photos that are GPS tagged. Later, you can upload them to the web and share them with friends.

Before you purchase a GPS unit, keep in mind that these devices don't pick up signals indoors, in heavily wooded areas, on mountain peaks, or in deep valleys.

Trip Planning

Planning your hiking adventure begins with letting a friend or relative know your trip itinerary so they can call for help if you don't return at your scheduled time. Your next task is to make sure you are outfitted to experience the risks and rewards of the trail. This section highlights gear and clothing you may want to take with you to get the most out of your hike.

Equipment

Since most name brands will differ only slightly in quality, it's best to know what you're looking for in terms of function. Buy only what you need. You will, don't forget, be carrying what you've bought on your back. Here are some things to keep in mind before you go shopping.

Clothes. Clothing is your armor against Mother Nature's little surprises. Hikers should be prepared for any possibility, especially when hiking in mountainous areas. Adequate rain protection and extra layers of clothing are a good idea. In summer a wide-brimmed hat can help keep the sun at bay. In the winter months the first layer you'll want to wear is a "wicking" layer of long underwear that keeps perspiration away from your skin. Wear long underwear made from synthetic fibers that wick moisture away from the skin and draw it toward the next layer of clothing, where it then evaporates. Avoid wearing long underwear made of cotton as it is slow to dry and keeps moisture next to your skin.

The second layer you'll wear is the "insulating" layer. Aside from keeping you warm, this layer needs to "breathe" so you stay dry while hiking. A fabric that provides insulation and dries quickly is fleece. It's interesting to note that this one-of-a-kind fabric is made out of recycled plastic. Purchasing a zip-up jacket made of this material is highly recommended.

The last line of layering defense is the "shell" layer. You'll need some type of waterproof, windproof, breathable jacket that will fit over all of your other layers. It should have a large hood that fits over a hat. You'll also need a good pair of rain pants made from a similar waterproof, breathable fabric. Some Gore-Tex jackets cost as much as $500, but you should know that there are more affordable fabrics out there that work just as well.

Now that you've learned the basics of layering, you can't forget to protect your hands and face. In cold, windy, or rainy weather, you'll need a hat made of wool or fleece and insulated, waterproof gloves that will keep your hands warm and toasty. As mentioned earlier, buying an additional pair of light silk liners to wear under your regular gloves is a good idea.

Footwear. If you have any extra money to spend on your trip, put that money into boots or trail shoes. Poor shoes will bring a hike to a halt faster than anything else. To avoid this annoyance, buy shoes that provide support and are lightweight and flexible. A lightweight hiking boot is better than a heavy, leather mountaineering boot for most day hikes and backpacking. Trail running shoes provide a little extra cushion and are made in a high-top style that many people wear for hiking. These running shoes are lighter, more flexible, and more breathable than hiking boots. If you know you'll be hiking in wet weather often, purchase boots or shoes with a Gore-Tex liner, which will help keep your feet dry.

When buying your boots, be sure to wear the same type of socks you'll be wearing on the trail. If the boots you're buying are for cold-weather hiking, try the boots on while wearing two pairs of socks. Speaking of socks, a good cold weather sock combination is to wear a thinner sock made of wool or polypropylene covered by a heavier outer sock made of wool. The inner sock protects the foot from the rubbing effects of the outer sock and prevents blisters. Many outdoor stores have some type of ramp to simulate hiking uphill and downhill. Be sure to take advantage of this test, as toe-jamming boot fronts can be very painful and debilitating on the downhill trek.

Once you've purchased your footwear, be sure to break them in before you hit the trail. New footwear is often stiff and needs to be stretched and molded to your foot.

Hiking poles. Hiking poles help with balance and, more importantly, take pressure off your knees. The ones with shock absorbers are easier on your elbows and knees. Some poles even come with a camera attachment to be used as a monopod. And heaven forbid you meet a mountain lion, bear, or unfriendly dog, the poles can make you look a lot bigger.

Backpacks. No matter what type of hiking you do, you'll need a pack of some sort to carry the basic trail essentials. There are a variety of backpacks on the market, but let's first discuss what you intend to use it for. Day hikes or overnight trips?

If you plan on doing a day hike, a daypack should have some of the following characteristics: a padded hip belt that's at least 2 inches in diameter (avoid packs with only a small nylon piece of webbing for a hip belt); a chest strap (the chest strap helps stabilize the pack against your body); external pockets to carry water and other items that you want easy access to; an internal pocket to hold keys, a knife, a wallet, and other miscellaneous items; an external lashing system to hold a jacket; and a hydration pocket for carrying a hydration system (which consists of a water bladder with an attachable drinking hose).

For short hikes, some hikers like to use a fanny pack to store just a camera, food, a compass, a map, and other trail essentials. Most fanny packs have pockets for two water bottles and a padded hip belt.

If you intend to do an extended, overnight trip, there are multiple considerations. First off, you need to decide what kind of framed pack you want. There are two backpack types for backpacking: the internal frame and the external frame. An internal frame pack rests closer to your body, making it more stable and easier to balance when hiking over rough terrain. An external frame pack is just that, an aluminum frame attached to the exterior of the pack. An external frame pack is better for long backpack trips because it distributes the pack weight better and you can carry heavier loads. It's easier to pack, and your gear is more accessible. It also offers better back ventilation in hot weather.

The most critical measurement for fitting a pack is torso length. The pack needs to rest evenly on your hips without sagging. A good pack will come in two or three sizes and have straps and hip belts that are adjustable according to your body size and characteristics.

When you purchase a backpack, go to an outdoor store with salespeople who are knowledgeable in how to properly fit a pack. Once the pack is fitted for you, load the pack with the amount of weight you plan on taking on the trail. The weight of the pack should be distributed evenly and you should be able to swing your arms and walk briskly without feeling out of balance. Another good technique for evaluating a pack is to walk up and down stairs and make quick turns to the right and to the left to be sure the pack doesn't feel out of balance. Other features that are nice to have on a backpack include a removable daypack or fanny pack, external pockets for extra water, and extra lash points to attach a jacket or other items.

Sleeping bags and pads. Sleeping bags are rated by temperature. You can purchase a bag made of synthetic fiber, or you can buy a goose-down bag. Goose-down bags are more expensive, but they have a higher insulating capacity by weight and will keep their loft longer. You'll want to purchase a bag with a temperature rating that fits the time of year and conditions you are most likely to camp in. One caveat: The techno-standard for temperature ratings is far from perfect. Ratings vary from manufacturer to manufacturer, so to protect yourself, you should purchase a bag rated 10 to 15 degrees below the temperature you expect to be camping in. Synthetic bags are more resistant to water than down bags, but many down bags are now made with a Gore-Tex shell that helps repel

The author backpacking with her dog Tiz. Photo credit: Ken Skeen.

water. Down bags are also more compressible than synthetic bags and take up less room in your pack, which is an important consideration if you are planning a multiday backpack trip. Features to look for in a sleeping bag include a mummy-style bag, a hood you can cinch down around your head in cold weather, and draft tubes along the zippers that help keep heat in and drafts out.

You'll also want a sleeping pad to provide insulation and padding from the cold ground. There are different types of sleeping pads available, from the more expensive self-inflating air mattresses to the less expensive closed-cell foam pads. Self-inflating air mattresses are usually heavier than closed-cell foam mattresses and are prone to punctures.

Tents. The tent is your home away from home while on the trail. It provides protection from wind, snow, rain, and insects. A three-season tent is a good choice for backpacking and can range in price from $100 to $500. These lightweight and versatile tents provide protection in all types of weather, except heavy snowstorms or high winds, and range in weight from 4 to 8 pounds. Look for a tent that's easy to set up and will easily fit two people with gear. Dome-type tents usually offer more headroom and places to store gear. Other tent designs include a vestibule where you can store wet boots and backpacks. Some nice-to-have items in a tent include interior pockets to store small items and lashing points to hang a clothesline. Most three-season tents also come with stakes so you can secure the tent in high winds. Before you purchase a tent, set it up and take it down a few times to be sure it is easy to handle. Also, sit inside the tent and make sure it has enough room for you and your gear.

Cell phones. Many hikers are carrying their cell phones into the backcountry these days in case of emergency. Keep in mind that cell phone coverage is often poor to nonexistent in valleys, canyons, and thick forest. More importantly, people have started to call for help because they're tired or lost. Let's go back to being prepared. You are responsible for yourself in the backcountry. Use your brain to avoid problems, and if you do encounter one, first use your brain to try to correct the situation. Only use your cell phone, if it works, in true emergencies.

Hiking with Children

Hiking with children isn't a matter of how many miles you can cover or how much elevation gain you make in a day. It's about seeing and experiencing nature through their eyes.

Kids like to explore and have fun. They like to stop and point out bugs and plants, look under rocks, jump in puddles, and throw sticks. If you're taking a toddler or young child on a hike, start with a trail that you're familiar with. Trails that have interesting things for kids, like piles of leaves to play in or a small stream to wade through during the summer, will make the hike much more enjoyable for them and will keep them from getting bored.

You can keep your child's attention if you have a strategy before starting on the trail. Using games is not only an effective way to keep a child's attention, it's also a great way to teach him or her about nature. Play hide-and-seek, where your child is the mouse and you are the hawk. Quiz children on the names of plants and animals. If your children are old enough, let them carry their own daypack filled with snacks and water. So that you are sure to go at their pace and not yours, let them lead the way. Playing follow-the-leader works particularly well when you have a group of children. Have each child take a turn at being the leader.

With children, a lot of clothing is key. The only thing predictable about weather is that it will change. Especially in mountainous areas, weather can change dramatically in a very short time. Always bring extra clothing for children, regardless of the season. In the winter have your children wear wool socks and warm layers such as long underwear, a fleece jacket and hat, wool mittens, and good rain gear. It's not a bad idea to have these along in late fall and early spring as well. Good footwear is also important. A sturdy pair of high-top tennis shoes or lightweight hiking boots are the best bet for little ones. If you're hiking in the summer near a lake or stream, bring along a pair of old sneakers that your child can put on when he wants to go exploring in the water. Remember when you're near any type of water, always watch your child at all times. Also, keep a close eye on teething toddlers who may decide a rock or leaf of poison oak is an interesting item to put in their mouth.

From spring through fall you'll want your kids to wear a wide-brimmed hat to keep their face, head, and ears protected from the hot sun. Also, make sure your children wear sunscreen at all times. If you are hiking with a child younger than 6 months, don't use sunscreen or insect repellent. Instead, be sure that his or her head, face, neck, and ears are protected from the sun with a wide-brimmed hat, and that all other skin exposed to the sun is protected with the appropriate clothing.

Remember that food is fun. Kids like snacks so it's important to bring a lot of munchies for the trail. Stopping often for snack breaks is a fun way to keep the trail interesting. Raisins, apples, granola bars, crackers and cheese, cereal, and trail mix all make great snacks. If your child is old enough to carry her own backpack, fill it with treats before you leave. If your kids don't like drinking water, you can bring boxes of fruit juice.

Avoid poorly designed child-carrying packs—you don't want to break your back carrying your child. Most child-carrying backpacks designed to hold a 40-pound child will contain a large carrying pocket to hold diapers and other items. Some have an optional rain/sun hood.

Hiking with Your Dog

Bringing your furry friend with you is always more fun than leaving him behind. Our canine pals make great trail buddies because they never complain and always make good company. Hiking with your dog can be a rewarding experience, especially if you plan ahead.

Getting your dog in shape. Before you plan outdoor adventures with your dog, make sure he's in shape for the trail. Getting your dog into shape takes the same discipline as getting yourself into shape, but luckily, your dog can get in shape with you. Take your dog with you on your daily runs or walks. If there is a park near your house, hit a tennis ball or play Frisbee with your dog.

Swimming is also an excellent way to get your dog into shape. If there is a lake or river near where you live and your dog likes the water, have him retrieve a tennis ball or stick. Gradually build your dog's stamina up over a 2- to 3-month period. A good rule of thumb is to assume that your dog will travel twice as far as you will on the trail. If you plan on doing a 5-mile hike, be sure your dog is in shape for a 10-mile hike.

Training your dog for the trail. Before you go on your first hiking adventure with your dog, be sure he has a firm grasp on the basics of canine etiquette and behavior. Make sure he can sit, lie down, stay, and come. One of the most important commands you can teach your canine pal is to "come" under any situation. It's easy for your friend's nose to lead him astray or possibly get lost. Another helpful command is the "get behind" command. When you're on a hiking trail that's narrow, you can have your dog follow behind you when other trail users approach. Nothing is more bothersome than an enthusiastic dog that runs back and forth on the trail and disrupts the peace of the trail for others. When you see other trail users approaching you on the trail, give them the right of way by quietly stepping off the trail and making your dog lie down and stay until they pass.

Equipment. The most critical pieces of equipment you can invest in for your dog are proper identification and a sturdy leash. Make sure your dog has identification that includes your name and address and a number for your veterinarian. Other forms of identification for your dog include a tattoo or a microchip. You should consult your veterinarian for more information on these last two options.

The next piece of equipment you'll want to consider is a pack for your dog. By no means should you hold all of your dog's essentials in your pack—let him carry his own gear! Dogs that are in good shape can carry 30 to 40 percent of their own weight.

Most packs are fitted by a dog's weight and girth measurement. Companies that make dog packs generally include guidelines to help you pick out the size that's right for your dog. Some characteristics to look for when purchasing a pack for your dog include a harness that contains two padded girth straps, a padded chest strap, leash attachments, removable saddle bags, internal water bladders, and external gear cords.

You can introduce your dog to the pack by first placing the empty pack on his back and letting him wear it around the yard. Keep an eye on him during this first introduction. He may decide to chew through the straps if you aren't watching him closely. Once he learns to treat the pack as an object of fun and not a foreign enemy, fill the pack evenly on both sides with a few ounces of dog food in resealable plastic bags. Have your dog wear his pack on your daily walks for a period of 2 to 3 weeks. Each week add a little more weight to the pack until your dog will accept carrying the maximum amount of weight he can carry.

You can also purchase collapsible water and dog food bowls for your dog. These bowls are lightweight and can easily be stashed into your pack or your dog's. If you are hiking on rocky terrain or in the snow, you can purchase footwear for your dog that will protect his feet from cuts and bruises.

Always carry plastic bags to remove feces from the trail. It is a courtesy to other trail users and helps protect local wildlife.

The following is a list of items to bring when you take your dog hiking: collapsible water bowls, a comb, a collar and a leash, dog food, plastic bags for feces, a dog pack, flea/tick powder, paw protection, water, and a first-aid kit that contains eye ointment, tweezers, scissors, stretchy foot wrap, gauze, antibacterial wash, sterile cotton-tip applicators, antibiotic ointment, and cotton wrap.

First aid for your dog. Your dog is just as prone—if not more prone—to getting in trouble on the trail as you are, so be prepared. Here's a rundown of the more likely misfortunes that might befall your canine friend.

Bees and wasps. If a bee or wasp stings your dog, remove the stinger with a pair of tweezers and place a mudpack or a cloth dipped in cold water over the affected area.

Porcupines. One good reason to keep your dog on a leash is to prevent it from getting a nose full of porcupine quills. You may be able to remove the quills with pliers, but a veterinarian is the best person to do this nasty job because most dogs need to be sedated.

Heatstroke. Avoid hiking with your dog in really hot weather. Dogs with heatstroke will pant excessively, lie down and refuse to get up, and become lethargic and disoriented. If your dog shows any of these signs on the trail, have him lie down in the shade. If you are near a stream, pour cool water over your dog's entire body to help bring his body temperature back to normal.

Heartworm. Dogs get heartworms from mosquitoes, which carry the disease in the prime mosquito months of July and August. Giving your dog a monthly pill prescribed by your veterinarian easily prevents this condition.

Plant pitfalls. One of the biggest plant hazards for dogs on the trail are foxtails. Foxtails are pointed grass seed heads that bury themselves in your friend's fur, between his toes, and even get in his ear canal. If left unattended, these nasty seeds can work their way under the skin and cause abscesses and other problems. If you have a long-haired dog, consider trimming the hair between his toes and giving him a summer haircut to help prevent foxtails from attaching to his fur. After every hike always look over your dog for these seeds—especially between his toes and his ears.

Other plant hazards include burrs, thorns, thistles, and poison oak. If you find any burrs or thistles on your dog, remove them as soon as possible before they become an unmanageable mat. Thorns can pierce a dog's foot and cause a great deal of pain. If you see that your dog is lame, stop and check his feet for thorns. Dogs are immune to poison oak but they can pick up the sticky, oily substance from the plant and transfer it to you.

Protect those paws. Be sure to keep your dog's nails trimmed so he avoids getting soft tissue or joint injuries. If your dog slows and refuses to go on, check to see that his paws aren't torn or worn. You can protect your dog's paws from trail hazards such as sharp gravel, foxtails, lava scree, and thorns by purchasing dog boots.

Sunburn. If your dog has light skin, he is an easy target for sunburn on his nose and other exposed skin areas. You can apply a nontoxic sunscreen to exposed skin areas that will help protect him from overexposure to the sun.

Ticks and fleas. Ticks can easily give your dog Lyme disease, as well as other diseases. Before you hit the trail, treat your dog with a flea and tick spray or powder. You can also ask your veterinarian about a once-a-month pour-on treatment that repels fleas and ticks.

Mosquitoes and deer flies. These little flying machines can do a job on your dog's snout and ears. Best bet is to spray your dog with fly repellent for horses to discourage both pests.

Giardia. Dogs can get giardia, which results in diarrhea. It is usually not debilitating, but it's definitely messy. A vaccine against giardia is available.

Mushrooms. Make sure your dog doesn't sample mushrooms along the trail. They could be poisonous to him, but he doesn't know that.

When you are finally ready to hit the trail with your dog, keep in mind that national parks and many wilderness areas do not allow dogs on trails. Your best bet is to hike in national forests, BLM lands, and state parks. Always call ahead to see what the restrictions are.

Day Hikes

- ☐ camera/film
- ☐ compass/GPS unit
- ☐ cell phone
- ☐ daypack
- ☐ first-aid kit
- ☐ food
- ☐ guidebook
- ☐ headlamp/flashlight with extra batteries and bulbs
- ☐ hat

- [ ] insect repellent
- [ ] knife/multipurpose tool
- [ ] map
- [ ] matches in waterproof container and fire starter
- [ ] fleece jacket
- [ ] rain gear
- [ ] space blanket
- [ ] sunglasses
- [ ] sunscreen
- [ ] swimsuit
- [ ] watch
- [ ] water
- [ ] water bottles/water hydration system

Overnight Trip

- [ ] backpack and waterproof rain cover
- [ ] backpacker's trowel
- [ ] bandanna
- [ ] bear repellent spray
- [ ] bear bell
- [ ] biodegradable soap
- [ ] pot scrubber
- [ ] collapsible water container (2–3 gallon capacity)
- [ ] clothing—extra wool socks, shirt, and shorts
- [ ] cook set/utensils
- [ ] ditty bags to store gear
- [ ] extra plastic resealable bags
- [ ] gaiters
- [ ] garbage bag
- [ ] ground cloth
- [ ] journal/pen
- [ ] nylon rope to hang food
- [ ] long underwear
- [ ] permit (if required)
- [ ] rain jacket and pants
- [ ] sandals to wear around camp and to ford streams
- [ ] sleeping bag
- [ ] waterproof stuff sack
- [ ] sleeping pad
- [ ] small bath towel
- [ ] stove and fuel
- [ ] tent
- [ ] toiletry items
- [ ] water filter
- [ ] whistle

Hike Index

About the Author

Lizann Dunegan is a freelance writer and photographer who specializes in writing outdoor guidebooks and travel articles about the Northwest. Her other books include *Best Bike Rides Portland, Oregon*; *Best Easy Day Hikes Bend*; *Best Easy Day Hikes Portland*; *Hiking Oregon*; *Road Biking Oregon*; *Hiking the Oregon Coast*; *Trail Running Oregon*; *Mountain Biking Oregon: Northwest and Central Oregon*; and *Canine Oregon*. Lizann has been hiking trails in the Northwest for more than 25 years and is often accompanied by her two dogs, Zane and Tiz. Lizann also loves trail running, cycling, and trail riding with her horses, backpacking, and camping.